SELL & MARKET YOUR BOOK

A Step-by-Step Guide

Daniel Cooke

authorHOUSE®

AuthorHouse™ UK Ltd.
500 Avebury Boulevard
Central Milton Keynes, MK9 2BE
www.authorhouse.co.uk
Phone: 08001974150

First published by AuthorHouse 4/2/2010

ISBN: 978-1-4490-7499-9 (sc)

This book is printed on acid-free paper.

AIMS OF THE BOOK

The purpose of this book is two-fold. Firstly, it is intended to help authors sell as many copies of their book as possible. Secondly, and as a result of healthy sales figures, it will serve to help authors raise their literary profile.

These two aims are self-perpetuating. The more copies of your book you can sell, the wider your readership. The more readers you have, the more your name will become known and your writing will be taken seriously. As readers recommend and review your book, this in turn will help to sell more copies, and so on.

The problem is often knowing where to begin, what steps to take and in what order. This book sets out the promotional tools available to you and advises you which paths are likely to sell the most number of copies of your book and which will help to establish your name as a published author.

Just remember that with each book that you sell, you will get closer to reaching critical mass, which is the stage at which your book will start to sell itself through favourable reviews and recommendations.

Unfortunately, books do not reach the market on their own. Rather, you have to introduce them into the marketplace, and encourage people to buy copies and read them.

It takes careful planning and know-how, and there is nobody better to promote your book than you. The more that you are actively involved in marketing your book, the better your chances of success.

CONTENTS

INTRODUCTION

This is a straightforward step-by-step guide to selling and promoting your book.

The marketing activities listed in the book are set out primarily in chronological order, in the order in which they should be done including pre-publication work and post-publication promotion over a three-year period. Depending on where you are in the publishing process, you can decide which chapter to start with in this book, and work your way forward.

The first step is always careful planning, so this book begins by explaining how to set up a marketing plan specifically tailored for your book.

Before your book is published, it would be helpful to design a website which promotes you and your book so that you can include the website domain name on all of your book's literature, e-mails, and so on. Also, having a website will provide another potential retail outlet for your book.

You then need to decide what supporting literature you might require for your future promotional activities such as letter-headed paper, posters, bookmarks and business cards.

Once your book is published, you can draft a press release and upload it to various PR websites and newswires, as well as send a tailored e-mail to relevant trade or literary groups inviting them to purchase and review your book.

About a month after your book is published, you may want to organize a formal book launch. It's important to decide the right venue for your launch and how much you should spend on it, as often authors spend their whole marketing budget and a lot of time on one big event, and a few weeks later, there's no further activity and so the momentum and sales built up from the book launch taper off.

The more you can convince your friends and family to help spread the word about your book and assist with media coverage and reviews, the better. Some (but not all!) of your relatives and colleagues will be happy to help – it's a matter of knowing what to ask them to do and how to ask them to do it.

E-mail marketing campaigns can be useful. Still, it can also be counterproductive, depending on how it is done. Similarly, advertising on the internet and in print media can generate leads and interest, but this should be well researched. I know one author who spent over £800 on a box advertisement for his book in *Time Out*, and it helped him to sell 3 more copies. That comes to around £265 per book, which is not money best spent when you consider that he could have paid for a decent website and some promotional literature for that amount.

Book reviews are useful both in terms of raising awareness of your book, and convincing people to actually buy copies. You can organize reviews for your book on Amazon and other websites which sell your book, and publications which specifically review self-published books. Seeking endorsements or recommendations from major book groups can also be useful.

Social networking both online and offline can be one of the most effective means of promoting yourself and your book. It is a just matter of targeting the right discussion boards, review websites and literary forums. Similarly, there are various groups and societies which authors can join which will provide them with a means to talk about their book with others who might help them with reviews, feedback and so on.

Depending on the type of book that you have published, many authors today are taping and uploading short videos which can be used as trailers for their books. Others are taping and selling their books in audio format, which is becoming much more commonplace today. Some samples are provided in this section of the book, along with free resources and effective video and audio platforms to achieve this.

Newspaper, magazine and radio coverage is discussed in the next section. The rule of thumb to follow is to start with your local press media, and then broaden out to regional coverage. Once those are achieved, then you can shift your focus to national and international coverage.

One of the main difficulties with marketing self-published books is getting them onto bookshelves in bookshops. This section tells you how to achieve this and what questions to expect and pitfalls to avoid. It often takes 4 – 6 weeks after the official publication date of your book before it shows up with an ISBN number on the computers at many bookshops, and it is essential to wait until it does appear before speaking with them. Meanwhile, any local press coverage that you can secure beforehand will increase your chances with the bookshops.

Similarly, most bookshops are reluctant to allow book signings for self-published books unless you're a local author, and even then it often takes some convincing. However, if you speak to the right person and say the things that he or she wants to hear, you can set up a book signing tour if you are determined for your book to succeed.

Talks at schools and libraries can also be useful both in terms of raising your profile and selling copies of your book. It is useful if you can focus on the central libraries and link your talks to a local bookshop which can provide copies of your book. Obviously, it is import that your talk be interesting and informative to your audience.

Other established venues for promoting yourself and your book include literary festivals, as well as trade shows and conferences. It is important to attend only those which are most useful.

Finally, there are well-publicized examples of unconventional means which some authors have employed to get press coverage. It depends to what extent you are prepared to go to sell yourself and your book. Imitating Lady Godiva may seem appropriate to some, but it might also land them in jail, and deservedly so.

As your marketing plan should be tailored around your personal knowledge, confidence, interests and abilities, the appendix to this book is comprised of a useful checklist which you can use in the step-by-step promotion of your book.

CHAPTER 1

Having an Effective Marketing Plan

Developing a clear marketing strategy to sell and promote your book is essential. It helps to clarify what you want to achieve and how to achieve it in the following ways:

- Your marketing plan will set reasonable goals which will give you a sense of progress and motivate you to continue with your promotional work.
- It describes the type of people who are likely to buy your book, and gives you a framework in which to build that readership.
- You marketing plan will prioritize your list of potential buyers and focus your promotional efforts to ensure that you reach your target market.
- It enables you to budget your time and money properly, and ensure that you meet important marketing deadlines and spread out the work for you, so you don't feel like you have to do everything all at once. It is important that your promotional work is done is stages, so that you

> do not have one big splash of publicity, and then lose momentum.
>
> • Finally, it is helpful to have a checklist so that you can keep track of what's been done, and what more needs to be done.

It is never too early to begin formulating a marketing plan for your book. In fact, the best time to prepare your marketing strategy is right at the beginning of the production stage because having an eye-catching front and back cover design, having a suitable blurb about you and your book on the back cover, and pricing the book accordingly are important when it comes to marketing your book.

It is also never too late to develop a marketing plan. The important point is that the earlier that you create one, the better equipped you'll be to sell your book.

What Do You Want to Achieve?

What is your main reason for writing and publishing your book?

1. Was it to help or entertain readers?
2. Was it to become known as a published author?
3. Was it to supplement your income or make a living from writing?
4. Was it because you wanted it to be part of your legacy?
5. Was it for some other reason?

If your primary aim in writing the book was to document an historical event or to share your life's experiences with your friends and family for posterity sake, then your marketing plan will involve much less time, money and effort than someone who wants to become an internationally recognized author, or authors who want to share their stories with everyone who might enjoy them.

The key to a successful marketing campaign is to set realistic expectations and to manage them appropriately. While you may want your book to be recommended reading on a mainstream talk show, or favourably reviewed in the *Guardian*, if you base your marketing plan around such high aspirations, then you are setting yourself up for failure because most TV shows and broadsheet newspapers do not recommend or review self-published books.

Similarly, if you aim to get your book into every bookshop in the UK, or expect to sell 10,000 copies in the first year, then you are probably setting the bar too high. Major book buyers and distributors like TBS and Gardners decide which books get into most bookstores, and few of these book buyers take on self-published books. This issue is discussed later in the section about Getting Your Book into Bookshops, and it would be much more realistic and effective to focus your time on local bookshops and regional representatives.

Some authors also think that if they throw enough money at it, their book will be a success. If you spend £1000s on a fantastic launch party, or buy hundreds of copies of your book which subsequently sit on your stairway, then you are not getting the results that you are seeking.

Finally, it is misguided to think that if your story is good or original enough, with a little marketing effort it will take the market by storm. Rather than planning for a storm, if you can make at least some waves with your promotional efforts, then that is reasonable start. And if you are not making waves, , you are probably not rowing hard enough.

If, on the other hand, you set reasonably achievable targets, identifying where best to devote your time and energy, then you will reach critical mass quicker and give your book every chance of literary and commercial success.

Who is Going to Buy Your Book?

Once you are clear about what you want to achieve and what you are *likely* to achieve, you then need to position your book within the market. This is all important because saying "my book will appeal to everyone" is tantamount to saying "I'm not sure who my main readership will be." It may be your book will have a wide readership, but it is important to focus your efforts on those readers who are *most* likely to buy your book.

You cannot sell your book to everyone, but you can try to sell your book to some, and the more you know about your potential readers including their spending habits and interests, the more likely they are to buy a copy of your book.

One useful way to position your book is to identify two or three other books you feel your book will sit comfortably alongside on the bookshelves once published.

The best way to do this is through a visit to your local bookshop. If you list a number of similar books off the top of your head, this often leads to authors positioning their book alongside well-known literary classics which may have been published years ago. But you're not selling your books years ago. You're selling your book now.

So, you should identify two or three books which have recently been published, say, within the last two years. The list of similar books does not need to include international best-sellers or Booker Prize winners, but they do need to be similar in content and style to your book. In fact, it is probably best if they are not world famous books because you are listing the books that your book will be competing with for market share, and if you set yourself up against the likes of *Lord of the Rings* or *Harry Potter,* then you are most likely setting yourself up for failure. Again, it comes down to having reasonable expectations.

To identify your main readership, you first need to decide which genre your book fits into. Often fiction novels cross over into different genres, which can make it difficult to position your book and define its potential readers. If, for example, your book is a political satire, it could be in the "Political" section, the "Humour" section or perhaps even in the "Contemporary Fiction" section. By going to your local bookshop, you can browse through various books in each of these sections to determine which section your book would most likely fit into, and then choose two or three contemporary titles from that section which are similar in style and content to your own book. Avoid listing similar titles from different sections of the bookshop in the expectation that your book would appeal to readers of all three sections. It might, but what we are trying to do is to identify the *most likely* readers/purchasers of your book, and the narrower the demographic, the better, at least to start.

Once you have identified which section of the bookshop (ie. which genre) your book best fits into, you should also look at which books are receiving the most promotion. Which of the books in your genre have prominent positions on the shelves? Which books have multiple copies piled up on tables often set out in each section? This tells you which books are currently selling the best.

Once you have properly positioned your book alongside a few other related titles, you need to find out who actually buys these books - not necessarily who reads them, but who *buys* them. For example, if you've written a children's book for 2 – 4 year olds, the main buyers of your book are not going to be children aged 2 – 4 years, but their parents, schools, nurseries, libraries, childcare organizations, and so on.

You then need to develop a profile of the most likely people to buy your book. When you are at your local bookshop, you should watch book browsers in the section where your book would be shelved and take down some notes (or if the shop is busy, you might want to make some mental notes and write them down soon afterwards). The more observant you are and the more accurate you can be in defining your potential book buyer, the easier it will be for you to sell your book to them.

Here is a checklist of questions that you might answer in your observational research of book buyers:

Are they primarily male or female?
What is their estimated age (you should have a 10 year age range at most)?
What ethnic group do you think they are in?
What religious organization might they belong to?
Where do they live, locally or out of town?
What is their likely profession?
What does their daily routine involve? (shopping, commuting, planning for work)

What life events might they be facing (eg. bringing up children, dating, marrying, divorcing, retiring)?
What newspapers and magazines do they probably read?
What TV and radio shows are they likely to watch or listen to?
What websites do they probably visit when surfing online?
Do you think they are looking to buy a book to read to relax and pass time, or are they looking for guidance and instruction manuals?
What organizations and associations might they belong to?
What are their interests likely to be (besides reading books)?

Prioritizing Your Book Buyers

Now that you are beginning to build up a profile of the people who are likely to buy your book, you then narrow it down further and identify your core market so that you know where to focus and begin your promotional activities.

Non-Fiction Books

If you have written a non-fiction book, then it is much easier to know where you might sell your book. For example, let us say that you have written a book called *How to Protect Your Children From the Dangers of the Internet*. The market for your book will include:

~ parents of children who regularly surf the internet or participate in blogging, forums and chat room
~ local schools

- local libraries
- child protection agencies
- children's charities
- youth clubs
- Scouting and Brownies organisations
- child-minding organisations
- nanny organizations
- child safety governmental organizations
- IT companies who provide parental control software and security tools

Once you have listed the types of people, groups and organisations that fall into your target market, you then need to prioritize them in terms of which are most likely to buy your book, and do some further research to find out how and where you might contact them to raise awareness of your book's publication and encourage them to buy a copy of your book, or better still, to place a bulk order for multiple copies.

Those potential book-buying individuals, establishments or organizations that will be higher on your list will depend on how well you think your book fits with their own aims and policies, how likely they are to buy your book and if so, how many copies they might buy, and how easy it is to contact them and how helpful and supportive they are likely to be. For example, charitable organisations tend to have limited budgets and are only interested in cash donations or a mention of their organisation in your book than buying copies or helping you publicize your book even with an endorsement or a mention in their literature. On the other hand, most local and central libraries and bookshops will be keen to help you organize talks and books signing if you know how to approach them properly and what to say (as explained in Chapter 15).

You should always start your promotional activities locally, and then once you have done your best to promote your book to those in your area, you can focus on regional, national and possibly even international coverage. Marketing your book locally will be much more cost-effective and fruitful than taking on the enormous cost and often overwhelming challenges of seeking national and international publicity and global sales early on. Again, this ties in with setting reasons goals and once you reach them, then branching out to a wider audience.

Your marketing plan is a work-in-progress. As you learn more about your target readership and their book-buying habits, you will become more successful when you eventually set your aims higher. And the more success you can achieve in your early promotional endeavours, the more confident and motivated you will be in carrying forward burning the shoe leather with book signings, talks to local schools and libraries, attending trade shows and literary festivals to promote your book, and so on. If you set your aims too high, then you are very likely to experience repeated set backs early and become discouraged and disinclined to follow through with your full promotional plan.

If you have access to and know how to surf the internet, it is an ideal means for sourcing information about relevant groups, organizations, events, bookshops, libraries, schools and media outlets in your local area, and their contact details.

Libraries can also provide you with media directories, lists of trade associations and a comprehensive listing of related journals and periodicals. This includes the annual *Media Directory* by Guardian Newspapers which can help to identify local radio, television and newspapers. Most libraries have directories that list contact details for professional bodies, businesses and trade buyers which in the case of publishing includes book wholesalers, printers, distributors and retailers, all of which play an integral role in helping your book to reach its target market.

Fiction Novels

It is generally easier to identify and target the core book buyers for a non-fiction book than it is to market a work of fiction. Still, it can be done, and if your fiction novel receives favourable reviews in the press and people start to recommend your book to others, then you book can be commercially successful. It is just a matter of focusing your promotional activities in a slightly different way.

Let us say that you have written a crime novel based in London and Amsterdam called *Double Dutch*. You have been to your local bookshop and identified the following contemporary books as being similar to yours:

> *The Apothcary's House* by Adrian Mathews
> *The Devil's Playground* by Stav Sherez
> *Looking for Mr Nobody* by Sue Rann
> *The Night Ferry* by Michael Robotham

You then watch the people who browse and buy books from their location in the bookshop, and begin to build up a good idea of the sort of people who might be interested in buying your book. The notes that you have taken down indicate that they are:

- Primarily males in their mid-twenties
- Often professionally dressed
- In fairly good health
- They look as if they might commute to work and/or travel internationally
- They might be looking for a book to read on their way to work or on the airplane in their travels abroad
- Some seem to be pressed for time, and most did not browse for long
- They look as if they might be buying a book for themselves rather than for someone else
- A few of them were carrying the *Times* or *The Guardian* newspaper

How do you take this eclectic list of characteristics and develop a promotional plan from it?

Firstly, you look for clues in this list of characteristics of where these people might spend their time. Where do young men in their mid-twenties like to go? Where do people in good health work out? Where do people who travel a lot spend their time? How do you sell your book to someone who is pressed for time?

In answer to these questions, you might list the following venues where these readers would probably visit in future where you might successfully sell your book:

- Bookshops (of course)
- Nightclubs & restaurants
- Expensive clothing stores
- Gyms and sporting centres
- Shops at train stations (newspaper outlets)
- Shops at airplane terminals

- Crime writing festivals
- Libraries

If you take out advertisements for your book either online or in newspapers or magazines, you will know better whom to pitch your book to and how to tailor the advertisement for this young professional, cosmopolitan market.

Now that you have some idea of where the people who tend to buy Anglo-Dutch crime thrillers like yours tend to frequent, you need to prioritize this list so that you can identify ways in which you can get your book in front of them to browse and hopefully buy.

In terms of the example provided, it seems unlikely that you will sell many copies in your local nightclub. Similarly, it is unlikely that diners or clothes shoppers are going to take the time to browse your book, assuming the restaurant or store let you sell your book in their establishment in the first place, which is unlikely.

Looking over the list above, it would be best to target bookshops, libraries, and perhaps make some enquiries about selling your book at your local gymnasium and arranging to speak at the Harrogate and Reading crime writing festivals. In fact, if you search for "UK Literary Festival" on Google, you will find an updated list of useful literary gatherings across the UK on the British Council website. This is a good example of how the internet can help you to locate suitable venues to reach your target market once you have identified who your core book buyers are and where you are likely to speak to them.

Budgeting Your Time and Money

Now that you have set realistic goals and developed a better understanding of your potential book buyers and where you might reach them, and prioritized accordingly, it is time to get down to brass tacks and decide on how much time and expense you are able to devote to the various parts of your marketing plan. Again, the aim is to start locally and gradually broaden your promotional efforts.

In an effective marketing plan, timing is essential. Most people plan to hit the ground running. As soon as their book is published if not beforehand, they plan to have a big splash early on, usually by way of a book launch, on the hope that if they can get enough people talking about their book, it might take on a life of its own. However, this rarely happens.

It is much more effective to pace yourself and drip feed the press. A successful marketing campaign is going to be a marathon - not a sprint, with sales of your book not in fits and starts, but with sustained sales over an extended period of time. If you try to accomplish too much, too soon, you will burn out before you even get started.

Let us say that you aim to sell 500 copies of your book in the first 6 months. It would be best if you could plan to sell 200 in the first month with a book launch and book signings, and then, say, 75 in the second month, 75 in the third month, 75 in month four, and 75 again in the sixth month. The key is to keep up the momentum and not to expend all of your effort and budget in the first month.

The sales life of the average book is 3 years, so your marketing campaign should extend over that full period of time. Most copies of your book will sell in the first year, so that is the timeframe in which you should budget, say, 50% of your time and money, and then 30% in year 2 and 20% in year 3.

You should coordinate your promotional work with the actual, not the expected publication date of your book. No matter how carefully your book publication and promotion is planned, something is likely to arise which will inevitably lead to delays, and there is nothing more frustrating than someone interested in buying a copy of your book, and for it not to be available.

Traditional publishers have the timing and subsequent promotion down to a science. They know the actual date in which your book is going to be published, and they will plan their promotional activities around that specific date. That is one of the reasons why it can take six months or more for traditionally published books to finally reach the bookshelves after the publisher has signing the contract with the author, whereas self-published books can often reach the market sooner, but the author has to remain flexible because their publisher, printer, and possible distributor and retailer can all cause unforeseen delays. This point is raised again in Chapter 13 when considering when is the best time to approach your local bookshops about the prospect of doing book signings.

Certain promotional activities can and if possible should take place before your book is published. You should start the process of creating a website for your book as explained in the next chapter so that it is up and running once your book is available to buy. You should also begin thinking about and sourcing the supporting materials that you might need when you are fully engaged in promoting your book (as outlined in Chapter 3). You can prepare the promotional pitch for your book which includes a short summary, an author bio, your book's USP (unique selling points), and being ready to tailor them to your audience. You can draft a press release to announce the launch of your book, and write down a list of PR websites and newswires which you plan to upload your book release to once your book is actually published (Chapter 4).

To maximize the sales potential that the internet offers with its global audience, you can sell your book on your own site and through other online book retailers (Chapter 5). There is a lot of preparatory work which needs to be done if you are planning on having a successful book launch (as described in Chapter 6), including asking your friends and family to help both with the book launch and after the book launch (Chapter 7).

Other promotion activities like direct marketing and paid advertising, turning your book into audio format, getting your book into bookshops, attending literary festivals and climbing Mt. Everest (Chapters 8 – 16) should be done after your book is listed for sale on Amazon and available to purchase in your local bookshop, and preferably completed within the first year of your book being published. In the subsequent two years, you should focus your efforts and time on maintaining current sales levels by broadening your market reach and getting your book into more bookshops and other retail outlets.

Putting Your Plan Into Practice

Now you need to put your plan in writing, and then into practice.

You should devote the first page to clearly defining and setting out your goals and expectations.

On the next few pages of your marketing plan, you should list 2 or 3 books that your book would sit comfortably alongside on the bookshelves once published. Then, you should list the characteristics of your most likely book buyers based on your bookshop research, and where you are likely to find and address them. Based on this list, you can then prioritize your list of book buyers and begin to develop a clear marketing strategy.

You can then decide where best to devote your time and money by setting out your actual monthly promotional plans over a series of pages, and then transfer the action points into a calendar or diary.

The next step is to read the rest of this book and develop an action plan tailored to your own expectations, budget and time commitments listing what you can do and when you plan to do it. To facilitate this process, there is a helpful step-by-step checklist in the appendix to this book which lists the promotional activities explained in the next 16 chapters.

Let us say that you expect your book to be published around mid-April, you can start with a section dedicated to January, a full three months prior, in which you outline the pre-publication marketing activities which you plan to do. If you are exceptionally well-organized, you should set out plans for the next 38 months.

If, on the other hand, your book is already in print, you can tailor your marketing plan accordingly. It is also never too late to develop your marketing plan, and the earlier that you do so, the more likely it will be that your book will fulfil its true potential and meet your literary hopes and aspirations.

Let us say that your book has just been published. Rather than starting with designing and developing a website which can take a while, you might want to focus on drafting a press release and uploading it to various websites as well as talking to your local newspaper about doing an article to get the ball rolling and to make sure that there is some initial press coverage. The point is you need to tailor the information about ways and means to sell and promote your books, as provided in this book, to suit your own schedule and abilities.

Keep in mind your marketing plan is always going to be a work-in-progress, as you will modify it as you see how your book is received by buyers and reviewed by readers. As you learn more about your book's prospects, you'll develop new and more effective ways to sell your book. If sales go well, you might want to reinvest some of the profits into more promotional opportunities.

If sales have slowed, you might want to reassess the situation and refocus your efforts, or reposition your book within the market. Perhaps you have exhausted the local market for your book and need to shift your focus earlier than expected on the wider book market.

Remember that any set-backs are always temporary when marketing your book. With careful planning and perseverance, you will gradually build up a steady readership for your writing and eventually attain the goals that you have set for yourself and your book.

CHAPTER 2

Creating a Website

The growth of the internet with its global reach and ready access to information has dramatically changed the way books are published and will be published in future. Although people still prefer reading printed books rather than having to read them off their computer screen, the fact that you can log-on to the internet and order a book from either Amazon or Barnes & Noble and it will (usually) be delivered within a week or two, or surf the internet and within minutes find out more about a book and its author, makes self-publishing more viable and selling self-published books much easier.

Moreover, the internet is the fastest-growing marketplace for books, with online sales predicted to surpass sales through bookshops and other traditional retail outlets within a decade. The fact is if you are a published author or soon to be one, you really should have a website which promotes you and your book, and designing one is much more affordable these days that you might think.

Setting Up Shop on the Internet

The first step in tapping into online consumer habits and technology is to create your own "home" or "shop window" on the internet. The design and content of your website will depend on your marketing goals. If your aim is to raise your literary profile, to build up your name as a recognizable and respected author, then the structure of your website will differ from a website which focuses on just one book that you've written.

Some authors, especially IT specialists, set up multiple websites for their writing to provide various shop windows to showcase their writing. Yet, this can be counterproductive because if you promote your site on your marketing stationery, or give out multiple www addresses to others, it could be confusing. Still, the more you know about website design and search engine optimization, the better positioned you will be to harness the power of the internet to market your book.

Firstly, you need to find someone who knows what they are doing to design a website for you. Your first port of call in this regard might be someone in the family who can design your website for you as a birthday or Christmas gift. Alternatively, if there are no website designers in the family, the next idea is to ask someone else whom you know who has published if they have a website and if so, whether they would recommend their website designer. The third option would be to check your phone directory for local website designers and compare costs, or if you know your way around the internet, the cyberspace abounds with internet companies. If you can find one that specialises in author websites, then that generally helps as they will have templates which they have used for other authors that will keep the cost down, and they will know what questions you are likely to ask and what issues are likely to arise. One website design company you might be interested in viewing is Book Promology (www.book-promotion.com).

A professional website designer will generally have their own hardware called a "server" which hosts websites. "Hosting" means reserving a space or bandwidth on their server which enable you to have your own website on the internet. The cost of annually hosting your website will be included in the website design and development package which they offer you. For example, let us say they quote £400 to create a website for you. This generally includes registering your chosen domain name, designing a basic website for you (which is all you need to start), and annual hosting of your website (there will be an ongoing annual charge for hosting). This might also include on-going maintenance to your site if you would like to make occasional changes to the wording on your website.

Depending how well-established the website designer is, they might try to sell additional services to you like tailoring your website so that when people search on the internet for subjects related to your book on various online browsers such as Google and Yahoo, they might find and accept your site (this is called "search engine optimization"). Or they might offer you e-mail campaigns or other forms of promotional support. If you follow the marketing advice offered in this book, you will not need your website design company to promote your book for you. You should be able to do it yourself and track your progress, which is important in learning more about your target readership and how to reach them. This is difficult to do when someone else promotes your website and your book for you.

As I mentioned previously, it would be better if you know someone, a friend or family member, who could create a website for you. They should be able to help you with registering your domain name, hosting your website and make any on-going changes at a substantially reduced rate.

Choosing Your Domain Name

The first decision you need to make is to select a domain name for your website, which will appear in its WWW (World Wide Web) address, or URL, which stands for Uniform Resource Locator (like the Quadratic Formula which you may have learned in Maths class in secondary school, you can forget this straight away because unless you are a contestant on Who Wants To Be A Millionaire, it is unlikely anyone is going to quiz you on what URL means).

As a general rule of thumb, the best author domain names tend to be the author's name or pen name, along with .com as the suffix. If the .com is not available, you might want to check whether .net is available. Also, the best domain names are short, easy to spell and descriptive of the site's content.

If your name is Janis Theresa Hick, for example, then you might select "JanisHick" as your domain name, so your website URL would be www.janishick.com. The problem is that the more common your name is, the more likely it is someone by that same name will have already registered your domain name. You might add in your middle initial, so your URL would be www.janisthick.com. The problem with this domain name is that it could be read as Jan Is Thick. With most names, however, you will not have this problem. This difficulty will be finding a domain name that is not already registered by someone with your same or similar name.

An easy way to check whether a domain name is available is to log-on to the internet and type in www.whois.co.uk. Type in your domain name of choice, click Order (this does not mean you are actually buying the domain name, but it simply moves you on to the next page), and see whether your domain name is available. If it says Yes, tell your web designer that you would like to register that domain name for your website. If it says No, you can click on Lookup to see who else has already registered that particular domain name.

If your name or the pen name that you are using is fairly common and most all variations on your name have been registered by someone else, then you might want to create a website that relates to the title of your book instead.

Either way, you should register your domain name in your own name, because the person who registers it legally owns that domain name. If you fall out with the person or company that set up your website, and they registered the domain name in *their* name, they have to agree to transfer it into your name which could create problems later. So, make sure that you tell whoever is registering your domain name that you would like it registered in your own name if possible.

Alternatively, it is fairly simple to register a domain name yourself if you are on the internet. Major online service providers like 123 reg (www.123-reg.co.uk) or Cheap Domain Names (www.uk-cheapest.co.uk) enable you to register a .com or .net domain name for £10 or less per year, and a .co.uk or .me.uk domain name for less than £5. They will also host your website annually for less than £20. Thus, you can organize your own domain name and hosting for less than £40.

There are some companies which offer you "free hosting", but it is often said, if it seems too good to be true, it probably is. There is always a downside. To receive "free hosting", the ISP (internet service provider) may require you to have banner ads or some other form of gaudy advertisement on your website that benefits the ISP but cheapens the look-and-feel of your literary website. Also, free website hosts will limit the amount of web space you get, usually to about 20 megabytes, and some limit the number of visitors you can receive in a month and if you exceed their "limit" your site will be "turned off" until the next month.

It might be worthwhile for you to register the .com or .net and the regional suffix for your website. If you live in the United Kingdom, then you might also register the .co.uk address and ask your website designer to redirect that domain name so that it points to your .com address, as that will help to avoid confusion if you give out your website address to others, and it will also avoid the possibility of someone putting in your domain name with a different suffix and bringing up a website that has nothing to do with your own site.

What Should You Put On Your Website?

You should design your website in much the same way that you might organize book proposals to publishers. You want to convey information about yourself and your book that is most likely to interest from your potential readers.

Look and Feel

Keep it simple and straightforward. Your website should have nice colours and be easy to navigate. One way to decide on what you would like your website to look like is to search the internet for other author websites, and pick one or two that you like. It is important to choose one which is suitable to your budget and expectations.

Let us say that you have written a crime thriller. You might start by putting the words "author of crime thriller" into your search engine such as Yahoo or Google, and scroll down a few pages, you will find plenty of websites to choose from.

Michael Connelly's website (www.michaelconnelly.com) is typical of a best-selling detective book author. You might point your website designer to this site and begin by including *some* of the categories listed down the left hand margin, as explained later in this chapter.

Or you might prefer the general look and feel of the Devon-based author Simon Hall's site (www.thetvdetective.com). By calling himself "The TV Detective", Simon is seeking to build a branding around himself as a writer of crime novels. This is another alternative to having your own name/pen name or the name of your book as your chosen domain name.

You do not need to have bells and whistles such as a Flash introduction for your website, as it tends to cost extra to design and can actually be a disadvantage as search engines cannot index images and graphics, and with Flash, they cannot even properly index the text embedded in the movie. A straightforward html website with literary-tailored content will suffice. When browsing the websites of other authors writing in your same genre, focus on the content rather than gimmicks or features.

Content

The most effective author websites are those which have more than just one page with their name and literary publications on it. This will give a shoddy feel to your website, and potential readers may assume that your writing is similarly amateurish. Still, you also need to balance this with the fact that the more pages that you have on your website, the most costly it is likely to be to design.

The best way to begin is somewhere between 5 and 10 pages for your website. You can always add more pages and functionality later as your book begins to sell and your marketing campaign grows.

Most visitors to your site will have heard you speak, read about you in their local newspaper, or possibly read one of your books. They may want to know more about where you come from and where you may be speaking next, or about other books you may have written and your inspiration for doing so.

In choosing the categories that you would like on your website, here is a short list of the essentials:

- ~ Home Page
- ~ About the Author
- ~ Books Published
- ~ Other Writings
- ~ News and Events
- ~ Contact the Author

The *Home Page* is the first page that visitors will see. It should be welcoming and introductory in the sense that you should not try to convey too much information straight away. On this page you should have detail about your writing in general. You might mention forthcoming talks or book signings that you may be doing in the next 3 - 6 months. If you do, keep in mind that you might need to keep your site updated by making periodic changes to this section, and depending on your website designer, there may be a small cost attached each time that you do this.

You should not have reviews of your books or endorsements of any kind on the Home Page as it will look like you are boasting or trying to convince visitors to your website that you are a good writer. If they have done a search for your site online, then you have already peaked their interest in your writing so you do not need to impress them with anything other than good quality writing.

On your *About the Author* page, you should avoid using the word "I" too often. You should talk about yourself and your writing in a way which might interest potential readers. You do not want it to sound too DRY (Don't Repeat Yourself). You might mention where you were born and grew up, what you do for a living besides writing, what your literary inspirations are, and what your hobbies are.

Your *Books Published* page is where you list the works that you have published, along with the cover designs for your books and a few lines about each of them. The books that you list should be links to the publishers' websites or to Amazon from which readers can buy a copy. You might also provide a few book reviews as links from their respective books on this page.

The purpose of the *Other Writings* pages is to showcase any other writing that you may have done such as short stories, poetry, published articles, and so on. These should be limited to a half dozen at most, like a literary portfolio rather than a literary library of your work. You want your website to highlight your best work, rather than seeking to impress visitors to your site by the fact that you're so prolific, especially if the majority of your work remains unpublished. Otherwise, the impression is one of quantity rather than quality writing.

The *News and Events* page lists press releases or newspaper or magazine articles about your writing, along with a list of upcoming speaking engagements. If you do any list upcoming talks or future book signings, it is important to keep your website content current. Be sure to change them once the events have passed. Similarly, if your contact details or publishing dates have changed, be sure that they have been updated on your website.

Some authors like to have an online diary in the form of a Web log, or more commonly known as a *Blog*, on their website. This enables them to keep a running commentary on their progress as a writer in publishing and promoting their book, and invite comments from others. Alternatively, some authors prefer to have a separate blog or video blog for their book, and link to it from their website, as discussed in Chapter 11.

It is essential to get *Contact the Author* page right. You should not mention any personal details on your website, like your postal address or telephone number. Rather, there are free "contact us" scripts which are simple and customizable so that visitors to your site can contact you via email without revealing your e-mail address, and SPAM spiders which scan pages for e-mail addresses will not locate your e-mail address.

You should find the right balance between promoting your work without hyping the book or boasting about your book's success. It does not add anything to post other author's quotes or glowing endorsements which say "this is one of the best books I've ever read" and "I cannot wait for the sequel". Too often, author sites are full of superlatives about how talented the author is or how exceptional the book is, from people with literary-sounding names and exotic foreign addresses, intended to give visitors the impression that their writing has global appeal and attained an international readership. As a good rule of thumb, the less the hype, the better the read.

Whatever you say on your website, it is essential that you get the details right! Otherwise, it would be like going to a job interview and providing incorrect or outdated reference details on your CV so even if the employer wanted to offer you the job, they would not be able to contact you or your references. Similarly, if you provide any e-mail or website links on your website which are broken or incorrect, or perhaps the details have changed since they were first uploaded to your site, these need to be checked regularly and corrected straight away.

Moreover, there is nothing more embarrassing that finding misspelled words on an author's website. After all, you are supposed to be the wordsmith! Many web designers will upload the website text you give to them without proofreading it for mistakes. After all, you've engaged them for their IT service, not for editorial services. And whereas it is difficult to pick up your own grammatical or wording mistakes, it might be useful to ask someone else to carefully read through the text prior to uploading it to your website, as well as after it has been uploaded to correct any mistakes because it is an easy assumption for readers and potential publishers to make that if you cannot spell well, then you probably cannot write very well. As unfair and untrue this assumption is – after all, Hans Christian Andersen and Agatha Christie were bad spellers with dyslexia – still, the more professionally presented your website is, the more inviting it will be for visitors.

Website promotion

There are a number of ways in which you can track visitors to your site, and sell your book to them. Firstly, you need to make it as easy for people to find your site. The can be done by optimizing your website for the major search engines.

Key Word phrases and search engine optimization

Search engines such as Google, Yahoo, Excite and AltaVista have "spiders" that scan the internet looking for key words and key word phrases from which they will rank or position your book when someone does a search on particular words which are found on your website. That is why it is important for your name to be prominent on your website, and preferably at the beginning of your text on the site. In web design terms:

- Every page on your site must have a unique HTML title tag, meta keywords tag, and meta description tag.
- Begin the body of your page with your keyword phrase, and repeat it a few times throughout

your site. For example, it might be "Kenneth King author" or "UK crime novelist."

- Feature your keyword phrase prominently by including it in headers and making it bold or in italics.
- Use the text navigation on your site and the keyword phrases that you have selected as links. Perhaps include a footer on every page using text links.
- If you break your site into various pages, link to the most important pages from every page of your site.
- Submit your site to The Open Directory and the Yahoo! Directory and build your link popularity by submitting your site to search engines, and requesting reciprocal links from related websites.

Reciprocal links

The more your book is mentioned on other websites, the better. If there are other authors writing about a similar subject, then you can e-mail them asking if they would be interested in putting a link to your website address on their site, and you would do the same for them. Or, let us say your book is a charming children's story about gnomes – a simple Google search on the word "gnome" brings up websites such as www.gnomeland.co.uk, www.gnomereserve.co.uk and www.gorrinthegnome.com, each of which might be interested if approached to provide reciprocal website links. In fact, you can link directly to the Amazon Recommends service which will list similar gnome-related books on your site.

Reciprocal links are useful in promoting your book because most search engines give higher positioning to your book if it is mentioned on various websites. The more others link to your site, the more likely that your book will come up in the first page of listings when someone does a search for, say, "books with gnomes".

Tracking visitors to your site

There are ways in which you can add tracking software to your website which enables you to monitor visitor numbers, and perhaps more importantly, which site the person visited immediately before coming to your site. This will tell you the sort of websites that it is most useful for you to link with. More sophisticated tracking software can tell you which country visitors to your site are come from, which can indicate whether or not your book would have international appeal.

Some website offer free hit counters and visitor traffic logs, but this information can be misleading as it can register "spiders" which simply trawl the internet for key word phrases and it can reflect visits from spamming specialists looking for e-mail addresses to add to their spurious databases. If you know how to read the data from these tracking devices, it might be interesting to see how many visitors there are to your site and whether that number is increasing with the marketing that you are doing for your book.

Pay-per-click advertising – pros and cons

It is possible to pay for banners which advertise your website to be placed on related websites, in which you pay the host a small fee each time someone clicks through to your site via that sponsored banner or sponsored link. This is called pay-per-click (PPC) and the largest network providers in this regard are Google AdWords, Yahoo! Search Marketing, and Microsoft adCenter. All three operate on a bid-based model - in other words, the more in-demand your key word or key word phrase is, such as "crime thriller", the more it can cost you each time someone clicks on your banner or advert link.

If your book is about a work of non-fiction about a unique person or a specific period in time, then PPC advertising might be worthwhile. For example, if your book is about the Cuban revolution in December 1956, then it might be worth investing a small amount and bidding on "Fidel Castro" or "Che Guevara" with Google AdWords. If you choose to promote your book in this way, make sure that you put a monthly limit on the amount paid for click-throughs.

There are various problems with this form of advertising for author websites. Firstly, it is open to "click fraud" which occurs when a site developer, automated script, or computer program imitates a legitimate click-through visitor. People are often put-off by adverts of this kind, and this can reflect badly on your book or literary profile. Finally, it is difficult to actually measure the effectiveness of pay-per-click advertising with author websites, and you should be careful not invest time nor money in something the results of which cannot be validated.

CHAPTER 3

Media Kit & Supporting Materials

Now that your website is done, you should put together a press pack which you can either reference immediately or send out to media sources when requested or required. The purpose of your press pack is to raise your literary profile and sell your book. This is basically a collection of relevant information about who you are and what inspired you to write the book, with useful reminders about the content of the book, what the press have said about the book, where people can purchase a copy and where you will be speaking or doing book signings next. It is essentially a printed version of your website.

Professional presentation is very important with your press pack. The more care that you take in putting it together, the more likely people will be to take your writing seriously and read and review your book. Put the enclosures together in a simple but nice folder, and organize the information in a way that makes the material easy to browse.

Your press pack should include:

- Cover letter, personalized for the recipient

- An author brief (include website address) & photo
- Fact sheet about your book (title, cover image, brief summary, publisher, ISBN, page count, publication date and price)
- Review copy of your book
- List of other published books
- Suggested interview questions & answers
- Media contact (whom they can contact with questions or interview requests)
- Endorsements from people the media will care about
- List of book signings & speaking engagements

You can also include:

- Current press release
- Past press clippings
- Sales figures (especially for past books)
- Info on your target market (who reads your books? who *buys* your books? This helps journalists know if your book appeals to their target audience)
- Extract from your book
- Bookmarks

The promotional pack should be tailored to the person to whom it is addressed. The cover letter should mention the person by name, and point out the benefit or particular interesting features of your book for the audience of the media source that you are sending it to. Similarly, the content of the kit should be customized to suit the recipient. For example, you should include an extract from your book or preferably a review copy, but not both. The media kit should focus on quality, not quantity, as you do not want to send too much material for journalists to sift through, especially if they are likely to be extremely busy.

When to send the Media Kit

Once your book is published, you want to "hit the ground running" with your promotional work. However, as explained in Chapter 12, you do not want to send out the press information too soon. Ideally your press pack should be sent out a month after your book is published. The reason is because when a book is published, if you have an ISBN number, most publishers will send your book's details to their distributors, who then upload the information to their "new publications" CD and send it out to their book retailers. The bookshops then have to upload this information to their computers. This can take anywhere from 1 – 4 weeks post-publication, and you should check whether your book is listed for sale on Amazon and on the computers at your local bookshop before seeking reviews, because you don't want to raise awareness of your book's publication, only for people to ask for it at the local bookshop and be told that it is not available.

Some self-publishing companies do not automatically pass on your book's details to distributors unless you pay them to do so. This is something you should check on with your publisher. The more distribution channels for your book, the more copies it is likely to sell.

If your book has been published by a traditional publisher, then you might want to wait until your book appears on the shelves at your local bookshop. Again, this can take some time, and it would be better to wait for the book to appear before sending the press pack for review to various magazine and newspaper journalists.

<u>Which Media Sources to approach</u>

You should focus your initial promotional activities on local and regional media outlets, then national and international media sources. You can find out more about local media sources at your local library, reading through back issues of newspapers and magazines. You can also compile a list of local and regional publications and contact them directly asking whether they might be interested in receiving a press pack and possibly reviewing your book. You should do your research before contacting them, rather than ringing them randomly. Make sure that you write down the name of a particular person to address your cover letter and press pack to.

Again, you should tailor the content of your press pack to the individual media sources. Most media sources will not run a story or do a review for your book simply because you ask them to do so, as they are not in the business of free advertising. Rather, you need to have a particular hook or angle for them to write about, and most focus on human interest stories or current affairs. In a later chapter, I discuss in detail how to secure press coverage in you local and regional newspapers, magazines and radio.

<u>Other Marketing Materials</u>

There are other ways in which you can promote your book without having to distribute a full media pack each time. For example, you might have letter-headed paper or flyers made up to promote your book to people you correspond with or for you to hand out at networking events, trade shows, talks and book-signings (more on this in Chapter 14). Business cards mentioning your name, contact details, book title and website address can also be useful. Similarly, postcard with this information on the back along with a picture of the cover design for your book on the front can also be effective. You might ask your local library if you can leave a stack of bookmarks on the front desk or on tables for people to pick up and keep. These should be professionally designed and printed to give the right impression about you and your book. You can often purchase these in bulk to keep the costs down.

In sum, other printed promotional materials could include:

- Letter-headed paper
- Promotional flyers
- Business cards
- Postcards
- Bookmarks

CHAPTER 4

Drafting & Uploading a Press Release

Writing an Effective Press Release

Once your book is published, you may want to draft a press release announcing the launch of your book which provides details about your book in brief.

This first press release should include a small photo of the front cover of the book, along with the book's International Standard Book Number (ISBN) which is a 13-digit number that uniquely identifies books published internationally. The purpose of the ISBN is to establish and identify one title or edition from a specific publisher and is unique to that book, allowing for efficient marketing of products by booksellers, libraries, universities, wholesalers and distributors.

The date when the press release is issued should be added above the headline, and the headline should include the name of your book and the author's name. This reason is because once the book is uploaded to various websites, this will increase the likelihood that your book title and name will be picked up by the search engines, as explained in Chapter 2.

There should be few paragraphs about the book, a brief about the author, and an action-filled excerpt from the book about a half page in length. Then, you should include a website address (preferably from Amazon) or two where the book can be ordered, and the publisher's or author's contact detail for any press enquiries.

Sample Press Release on Publication

Here is a sample press release for this book which can be used as a template:

FOR IMMEDIATE RELEASE
10th January 2010

Exciting New Fantasy Novel entitled MAGICAL REALMS by Steve Jones is published

About the Book:

In the magical realms, there is a fine line between Magic and reality. Magic conceals its presence from reality, and only a few can see it. Gradually Magic revealed itself in people, enabling things to be achieved that we never thought possible before.

One day, the King banished all those who embraced and practiced the Magic, and sent them out of the Kingdom. They were sent to the land of Rocks, and turned the land into the land of precious gems. Soon, the people in the Kingdom were jealous of the Magical Land, and set out to push the inhabitants further to the outer reaches of the Kingdom so that they could have the diamonds, rubies and other precious jewels. The people of the magical realm, however, decided that they would defend their land against the invaders – this is their story.

About the Author:

Steve Jones lives in Northumberland in England. He has worked in the construction industry for over 20 years before turning his hand to writing. Steve is currently working on his next fantasy novel set in the Magical Realm.

Excerpt from the Book:

"The people of the Kingdom pursued Muriel through like a hunter after its prey. But Muriel was relentless and without fatigue. The more they advanced, the more determined she became.

The Kingdom people cornered Muriel and she was forced to reveal her Magic. She created huge rocks out of the gas and dust and hurled them at the people who avoided them. Muriel summoned its vast energy and threw a burning rock at them but again, to no effect. Then they moved closer and enveloped the desperate force. Muriel wrapped herself in the tiny particles of gas and dust and hid there fearful of its existence, hindered only a moment by the final hail of stones that could divert it from its purpose and then she moved forward."

A copy of this book can be ordered from [publisher name] at:
http://www.publisher-name.co.uk/BookStore/ItemDetail-bookid-11111.aspx

and from Amazon.co.uk at:
http://www.amazon.co.uk/Steve-Jones/
ref=UTF8&s=books =8-1

Media Contact:
Publisher:
Tel.:
e-mail:

Distributing Your Press Release

You should include copies of the latest press release in your press pack. To sell your book and raise your literary profile, there are a number of free PR website and online newswires where you can upload your press release, and details on each of these sites on how to do so. Here is a list of sample sites that you might upload your press release to:

www.pressbox.co.uk
www.free-press-release.com
www.i-newswire.com
www.24-7pressrelease.com
www.clickpress.com
www.express-press-release.com
www.prlog.org
www.freepressreleases.co.uk
www.freepressindex.com
www.free-press-release-center.info
www.nosyjoe.com
www.sanepr.com
www.your-story.org
www.pr.com

It usually takes 2 - 3 days before the press releases appear online as some PR websites may want to check them firstly before uploading them.

About a week after you have uploaded your press release to these sites, you can put your book title and name into a Google Search and it should bring up about a half dozen of the press releases.

If your e-mail address is listed on the press release, you might receive confirmation e-mails from some of these PR websites and newswires saying that your press release has been approved or notifying you if there is a problem with them. You might also receive an offer or two from sites linked to the free websites inviting you to pay for positive reviews and further promotion. You should simply delete these e-mails as they do not do anything that you cannot do yourself.

You can also e-mail or send copies of your press release to various "Writers' Circles, Literature Courses and Workshops" listed in the Directory by same name which can be found on www.writers-circles.com, tailoring the press releases and inviting them to read and review your book.

Drip Feeding the Press

Rather than issuing one press release only about the publication of your book, you should drip feed the media with periodic press releases that stimulate public interest and invite reviews and interviews. You can write book releases about upcoming speaking engagements, festival talks, future book signings, success in writing competitions, and any other newsworthy events linked to your book in particular.

In these press releases, your first few paragraphs should clearly explain who and what the release is about, when and where the upcoming event will take place, and why the event is important and worth noting. Keep in mind that your press release is intended to generate news, and it probably will not be reprinted word-for-word.

In terms of do's and don'ts for press releases:

- **Do** be as clear, concise and compelling as possible
- Do invite reviews for your book and interviews of yourself
- Do include your website address
- Do check and double-check spelling, dates and contact details
- Do keep it to one or two pages at most

- **Don't** hype your book or overstate the relevance of the event
- Don't word your press release like an advertisement, saying something like "special offer on bulk orders"
- Don't have fancy designs or frames around the text
- Don't use clichés like "the next best-seller" or as an example from Amazon: "Thought-provoking, life-affirming, triumphant and tragic, this is a novel of breath-taking scope, masterfully told.... A wonderful page-turner."

CHAPTER 5

Selling Your Book Online

Selling books on your website

To maximize the sales potential that the internet offers with its global audience, you can sell your book on your own site and through other online book retailers.

Let's say that you would like to buy 100 copies of your book from your publisher (presumably at a discounted rate as the author) and sell them yourself via your website to maximize the margin that you'll receive for each copy sold. You can set up a "click here to order" link which enables people to contact you directly by phone or by e-mail to place an order, or you can set up an e-commerce facility through a transaction provider such as Worldpay or Paypal and automate the purchase so that you only have to be involved in fulfilling any orders by actually sending the books to the customer once the order has been placed.

Direct sales

The benefit of the "click here to order" link is that you would not have to pay a commission on each sale to the transaction provider, and that it provides a more personal touch when someone does order a copy of your book via your website. However, there are a number of downsides as well. Firstly, there is the privacy issue. When you take and fulfil any book orders yourself, you have to stock a number of copies, and you will need to tell people where to send payment which, unless you have a warehouse, business address or PO Box, means disclosing your personal address to others which is potentially risky.

Also, there is the time-management issue, as you will have to be involved right from the outset in any book order, which can take time and effort. You will need to acknowledge the customer's order request and tell them where to send payment and how much they need to send to cover the cost of postage. You then need to wait for their payment to arrive and clear, which can take a while and delay fulfilment of the order. You will also need to follow up once the payment has cleared and tell the customer when the book has been sent.

If you have self-published your book and you are planning on selling most of the copies to trusted friends and family, this is probably your best option because it is more personal and you can thank them yourself for buying copies. Also, it reduces the additional costs of having to pay for the initial set-up and on-going commission from any sales to a middle man, in other words, to the transaction provider.

Automated sales

If you are aiming to sell multiple copies of your book to a much wider audience who might be interested, then you might consider setting up an automate system whereby people can place orders for your book. Selling online in this way is known as electronic commerce, or "e-commerce" for short. This would require you or your web designer to link your site to an established payment system such as Worldpay. As I mentioned, there is generally a set-up fee for linking to them, much like you would pay the phone company to set up a telephone line for you in your house. Also, each of these transaction providers will take a small cut from each sale, and their "cut" will depend on the level of service they provide. Again, it is like paying a standard rate for each phone call that you make. The transaction provider will deduct a certain amount as per their service agreement with you for each book sold through their shopping cart facility on your website.

The main benefit of having an e-commerce facility on your site is that everything is automated, including the financial transactions, and you will receive payment from the transaction provider every month or quarter. Also, it enables people to order copies of your book on their credit cards, which makes it easier for them and thereby could lead to more sales.

The difficulty, of course, is that they will take a nibble out of your earnings for every sale, and they charge you upfront for the privilege! Also, there is likely to be an annual cost for retaining the service, which could cost more than the margin you are making by selling books in this automated way on your website. Still, if you're planning on actively promoting your book, then this is probably the best way for you to maximize sales.

In fact, you can set up your website so that people can contact you directly if they would like to order a copy of your book but do not want to give their credit card details online, or they do not have a credit card, or they prefer to send payment by post. Or, if your site is set up for e-commerce, then they could choose to pay directly via their credit card. By providing both options to customers, you will be increasing the likelihood that they will order a copy of your book. The easier you can make it for people to order copies of your book on your website through a personalized link or automated link, the more copies you are likely to sell.

Deciding which is best for you

If you have published a trade book or work of non-fiction that is likely to have a specialized market, or if you are an established author with many publications to promote on your website, then having both a direct link and automated link would most likely suit you best.

If, on the other hand, your book is a novel and you are a new author, then it is probably best to have a direct link on your website, perhaps with a link to other online booksellers such as Amazon who will also sell your book and take their margin for each sale.

Selling books via online retailers such as Amazon

Which websites currently list your book for sale

It seems obvious that most publishers would automatically list their authors' books for sale on their website, and preferably at least three months prior to publication to encourage any pre-sales activity. Yet, some publishers are belated in doing so, and need a gentle nudge from the author in this regard.

Also, some smaller publishers do not even have a website, which is surprising in this digital age, so it is even more important to ask them to upload your book for sale on as many third-party websites as possible.

If you have self-published your book, most people who buy copies will purchase them on Amazon, Barnes & Noble, Booksmart and other major online retailers. Nearly all traditional publishers and most self-publishing companies will upload your book for sale for you on these sites. A useful website to find out which sites are selling your book is www.bookfinder.com. Simply put your published name into the search facility and/or the title of your book, and it will bring up a list of which major e-tailers currently list your book for sale.

You should follow this up with a search on the sales portals that are listed to make sure the information provided about your book on them is accurate and current. It is surprising how many times these listings are obsolete, inaccurate, or lack an image of your book cover, all of which can be easily remedied.

You should check whether your book is for sale on other Amazon sites around the world. If, for example, you have written a novel about the American Civil War, then you should make sure that it is listed for sale on Amazon.com as well as Amazon.co.uk. Do not assume that because your book is listed on one Amazon site, it is listed on every Amazon site around the world because this is rarely the case because someone (presumably your publisher) has had to upload your book listing manually to each international site.

Uploading your book to Amazon

The largest and most widely known online bookseller is Amazon. If your book is not currently listed for sale on the Amazon site for your country (in the UK, this would be Amazon.co.uk), then you should either contact your publisher asking them if they plan to do this for you, or you can submit your book yourself for inclusion on these sites.

You (or someone you know who is a bit more IT savvy) can upload your book to Amazon UK by going to www.amazon.co.uk and clicking the "Sell Your Books" link in the upper right hand column of the menu bar. This will take you step-by-step through the process of setting up a merchant account for your book.

You will need an ISBN (International Standard Book Number) which is a unique, 13-digit numerical commercial book identifier for booksellers and stationers to categorize and locate your book. Traditional book publishers will automatically assign an ISBN to your book, as will most self-publishing companies. But, there are some self-publishers like Lulu.com where you have to pay extra for an ISBN number to be assigned to your book. If you are serious about selling your book and want to get it into retail bookshops and listed for sale on various online sites, then you must have an ISBN assigned to your book for distributors and retailers to be able to sell it, for librarians to order and stock copies on their shelves, and for Nielsen Bookscan to accurate register actual sales figures.

Amazon "Search Inside" program

One of the best free services that Amazon offers authors and publishers is the "Search Inside" feature which allows readers to peek inside and read a small amount of text before deciding whether to order a copy. It helps increase sales and can be a useful marketing tool because when customers search for books on the site, Amazon uses not just the author, title, and keywords provided by the author or publisher, but also the words from inside participating books to return the best possible selection of books in their search results.

To add this feature to your book's listing, firstly search for your name or the title of your book on www.amazon. co.uk. Under the picture of your book, click the link that says "Publisher: Learn how customers can search inside this book." You will be directed to a page that explains the benefits of the Search Inside program for authors and publishers.

The next step is to complete the registration form. You must be the exclusive rights holder - copyright and marketing/promotional rights - of the book that you want to submit to the programme. Once completed, you will receive an email explaining how to submit your book to the programme. You will need to provide the ISBN of the book and provide Amazon with a physical or electronic copy of your book. You can send PDF files, which is recommended to avoid shipping and handling costs, and to reduce the time it takes to get the book into the Search Inside programme. It generally takes three to five weeks for Amazon to upload a PDF file, whereas it can take six to eight weeks for Amazon to scan in and upload a physical copy of your book.

To send PDF files, you need to respond to the email you receive, indicating that you want to get a Seller Central or Merchant Account so you can upload PDF files to the Search Inside program. You will get a response with an attachment that includes guidelines and instructions for PDF submissions. You must upload the complete book in order to participate in the Search Inside programme, even if they only let customers preview a small number of pages. The reason for this is so they can provide optimal search functionality for a given book.

Listing your book for sale on third-party sites

Selling your book though other website portals or "online shop windows" can be particularly effective for books that are genre-specific or ones which have a specific target market such as trade publications. Cookbooks, hobby and craft books, local history, and genealogy books are some example of publications that are ideally suited for third-party sales and promotion.

Identify which websites (other than Amazon) are suitable to list your book

Other sites which may agree to list your book for sale, and take a margin for any orders placed, are major book retailers such as Barnes & Noble, Play.com, Ebay, Borders, Booksamillion.com, Pickabook.co.uk, Blackwell.co.uk, Powell's Books, and Half.com. Each of these online book retailers will have its own policies and procedures in order to carry your book. The larger ones work on a volume basis which means they might offer a discount on the recommended retail price of your book and receive a smaller margin per book, but they will make up for this by selling more copies than their competitors, or having expensive postage and handling costs.

You should check with your publisher which of these sites they plan to upload your book to and soon after your book is published, check on Bookfinder.com to see which of these booksellers already list your book for sale. Whereas Barnes & Noble will generally list your book for sale, if you would like to list your book for sale on Ebay, you have to upload it for sale yourself. It goes without saying that the more sites that list your book for sale, the more copies it is likely to sell. As a minimum you need to ensure that your book has an ISBN and that it is listed for sale on Amazon and Barnes & Noble.

Link via your website

If your book is listed for sale on, say, a half dozen online book retail sites, which of these (if any) should you link to on your website, and how should the listing read?

Some author websites provide links to every possible online retail site that lists their book for sale. The impression this gives is that they are trying to impress visitors by saying "look how many sites list my book for sale, it is sure to be a bestseller" in much the same way that one likes to see his or her book on the shelves in bookshops on the high street. There is no need to link to any other third-party sites besides one or two, namely whichever one the author feels best displays the book, or whichever one offers the largest discount for copies of the book, including postage & packing.

As a general rule of thumb, if your book is listed for sale on your publisher's website, it is usually best to link to your book listing on their website. This will cut out the middle man (the online bookseller) and the margin paid to them as a third-party retailer. You can also link to Amazon if there are positive reviews of your book on the Amazon site.

CHAPTER 6

Organising a Book Launch

The first step in organizing a book launch is to be clear about your objectives for the launch. These generally include:

- Enhancing your reputation and visibility
- Recouping your publication costs
- Celebrating a milestone in your career

When choosing the appropriate venue, whom to invite, what food and drink to provide, whether to do a book reading and signing, and whether to give a speech, the book launches that tend to work best are those that serve all three of these objectives.

The launch is an integral part in your marketing campaign. However, one mistake many authors make is that they splash out and spend the majority of their marketing budget on the launch, and then do not follow it up with further promotional activities. When figuring costs in your marketing plan, you should devote 20% of your marketing budget at most to your book launch, and the remaining 80% to putting together your marketing kit and sourcing supporting materials, organizing other functions such as book signings, social networking and attending relevant literary festivals, conferences, book fairs and trade shows.

If your book is about local regional or national history or trade-related, then you might consider seeking sponsorship for your book from your local chamber of commerce, or from professional organizations mentioned in your book. Let us say that your book takes place in Whitby and is about local legends and lore which bring tourists to the area. Your local tourist board might be willing to help sponsor and even promote your book launch if you contact them well in advance.

<u>The Venue</u>

You need to choose whether to hold your book launch in a private residence or public place. There are advantages and disadvantages to either choice. A book launch at home or at a friend's house is often the "safer" option as it is more personalized and often attended primarily by local friends and family. Author Anjali Mittal hosted the book launch for her children's book *The Convent Rules* at home because it was more relaxed. Anjali sent personalized invitations to friends and relatives, local school heads, local bookshop personnel, her local writers group, the local newspaper, the MP of the town and even the Mayor. She organized many areas of the house according to the theme of the party. There was a secret den, a haunted den, matron's cubicle, etc. The children thought it was great fun. She placed books and related items around the house where they would be visible, and put up posters and enlarged reviews of the book so people could read what others had written about her book.

If you hold your book launch in a more public setting, it can give your book a wider hearing and opens up the prospect that your event might be attended by others within the media industry who can raise awareness of your book's publication with reviews after the event. However, there can be extra costs involved in renting the room, and people tend to come and go more often which can make the room seem empty at times. It is more difficult to manage and avoid unforeseen eventualities like uninvited guests joining the party.

Whether you decide to hold a private, invitation-only book launch at your home or in a local pub, club or restaurant, or a more public event at your local library or bookstore, let your book inspire the theme of the event. If you've written a fantasy book, deck the halls with wizards, castles, dragons, and have the food, music and drink reflect it. If you have written a Jilly Cooper-style sex romp novel, however, it is probably best not to get too carried away.

Guest List

Create a one-of-a-kind invitation for the launch. You can design and print your own, or better still, invest in good quality invites for the party. It is best to have a high quality picture of your book on the invite so people register it and remember what it looks like. Request to RSVP.

Everyone on the guest list should be invited for a purpose, and invitations should go out at least three to four weeks in advance.

Guests should include:

- Close friends and members of your family

- Local arts council members
- Writers from local societies and reading circles
- Local school educators
- Library and bookstore personnel
- Local newspaper journalists

It is difficult to know how many people will turn up on the day, so make the premises sufficiently accommodating but not so large that guests feel that a lot of people did not show. Many people will reply to your invitations if they are professionally done, which will give you a better idea of expected numbers. As a rule of thumb, you should plan for half of those whom you invite to show up on the day.

Remember to prepare a news release to mark the event and forward it to your local newspaper four to six weeks in advance. Also, it is a good idea to send a personal invitation to your local newsperson, and follow up by contacting them a week or so later encouraging them to attend.

Practicalities

1. If you are holding a book launch at a venue in town or in the city, then Tuesday or Thursday evenings from 5:30 – 7:30 p.m. is probably best so people can come directly after work.

2. If you are holding a book launch at home, then weekend book launches are generally better attended. The time of day has a lot to do with the theme and your budget for the event. It could easily be a wine and cheese function or a masquerade event during the evening.

3. Have plenty of food and drink around for the duration of the party. Champagne is a good idea if you are going to

have a toast after the speech. If you can afford caterers to do the serving of food and drink, that will take pressure off you so you can concentrate on talking to guests. If not, get some friends to serve the food for you. Your image should be of a serious writer and not someone preoccupied with preparing food and running around serving others.

4. Designate someone who is a good photographer to take plenty of pictures or video the event. The pictures or video will be useful for promotional materials, websites and blogs.

5. The first half of the party should be devoted to greeting and socializing with guests. Be sure to welcome everyone and thank them for coming.

6. Midway through the party, or when you think the important people are present, you should make a short speech. Get someone to formally introduce you and say a few words about you before you start speaking. This has to be someone confident, who knows you well and has been a mentor in your journey. It is a great help when someone like that is standing by your side when you are doing your speech.

7. When you speak, thank people, say a bit about what inspired you to write, what the book is about and the success of it so far, and tell them what your plans are for your next book.

8. For a children's story, you might want to create a game or contest based on your book after your speech.

9. Another idea would be to get some local drama students to re-enact a scene from the book, film it and then place it

on your website and YouTube as a book trailer. The drama students will help you to promote your book each time they show the video to others.

10. Make sure there is a separate area where books can be signed and assign a person to sell the books for you as you will be busy mingling. Some pre-signed books are a good idea and always keep plenty of change.

11. Unless a close friend, what you write in the book should be something simple like "Best wishes to…. followed by their name, your signature and the date." Ask again if you don't catch the name exactly.

12. Send "Thank You's" to those who attended your book launch.

13. Write to the local newspaper after the event and tell them how the launch went and send them some pictures – you never know, they may print them!

CHAPTER 7

Mobilising Friends & Family

As mentioned previously, when promoting your book, you should start locally, then regionally, then nationally before eventually conquering the world.

A good example of this is vicar-turned author G. P. Taylor and his book *Shadowmancer*. When he completed the manuscript, Reverend Taylor was told that no publisher would be interested in a parable about Christianity and Black Magic set in the 18th century. He decided to ignore the naysayers and publish the book himself for £3500. He sold his Harley-Davidson to help cover the cost of self-publishing the book, and the novel's popularity spread primarily by word-of-mouth as parishioners, friends and neighbours recommended it to fellow readers.

This local groundswell of support and positive reviews and media coverage eventually lead Faber & Faber to offering to publish the book, which then spent 15 weeks at the top of the British book charts, making Rev. Taylor a millionaire and much sought-after literary talent. He sold the US rights to his book for £314,000 which is said to be more than three times J K Rowling's US advance for the first Harry

Potter story. He then signed a four-year deal for £3.5 million with Faber in the UK and Putnam in the US. The film rights to *Shadowmancer* were sold for £2.25 million, and his book has now been translated into more than 20 different languages.

The lesson of this story is don't underestimate the importance of viral (word-of-mouth) marketing. You may not have 80 parishioners and God on our side to strengthen your resolve in the marketing of your manuscript, but you will find that your nearest and dearest are often glad to help endorse, review and recommend your book if you can pluck up the courage to ask, and ask in a personalised way.

The best way to involve your family is to divide up the various sales and marketing tasks between them according to their level of interest, availability and contacts. For example, your children might be able to tell their classmates about your book, or perhaps your spouse could check with the local bookshops about ordering in copies of your book. One of your relatives might be proficient in IT and could help organise a website for you. They might be able to help by drawing up and distributing posters around local and central libraries. If you decide to have a book launch, they can help with the invitations, decorations and any performances on the day.

Friends are often an overlooked and underutilized resource for book promotion. We're often reluctant to impose, despite sincere offers to help toot their talented friend's horn. Invite friends personally to your next book event in their area. A personal invitation conveys the event's importance, as well as the valued friend's importance to you. Ask each friend to bring someone who doesn't know you.

Create "tell-a-friend" postcards and bookmarks - put your book cover on the front with the book's title, author, ISBN and your website address. A simple promotional message should go on the back like "This wartime romance novel is the perfect vacation read." Ask friends who have read your book to kindly give a few postcards to their friends and colleagues.

Befriend your local librarian and enlist his or her help. Create a postcard message encouraging the recipient to visit the library for the book. Ask check-out librarians to slip your book markers inside other crime novels when they are taken out. If the library doesn't stock your book, then submit a press packet – including a handful of postcards – to the librarian and ask them to order your book.

In your e-newsletter, ask recipients to send a "tell a friend" email. Provide text they can copy-and-paste into a new email (e.g. *check out my author friend's new blog. Here's the opt-in link to her mailing list)*. Email from a known recipient is less likely to end up in someone's spam folder, and a personal recommendation carries more weight than a general e-mailing to more than one person at the same time.

Ask friends with children if they're interested in recommending the book to be read in class (depending, of course, on the subject matter). If you have the time, you can offer to read the book to the class yourself, and then ask whether they can mention your book in the next parents' newsletter.

Encourage friends to recommend your book to other readers, to any groups or clubs they belong to, and to mention it in any newsletters or promotional materials that they send to their employees or to the general public.

Ask friends over for a promotional party – nothing like a little wine to get the ideas flowing! This can be more low-key than a full launch party, and it'll get friends talking about your book. Tell them that you would welcome any feedback on the book because that can often incentivise them to read it, and give them the sense that you really value their involvement.

Almost everyone has a network of friends who would be glad to help if they only knew how and are asked kindly to do so. Social networking on Twitter, Facebook, MySpace and personal Blogs as explained in Chapter 10 are excellent means to achieve this. Twitter (http://twitter.com) is a free service enabling its users to send and read messages known as *tweets*. Tweets are text-based posts of up to 140 characters displayed on the author's profile page and delivered to the author's subscribers who are known as *followers*. Senders can restrict delivery to friends or they can allow open access. Users can send and receive tweets via the Twitter website, text-messaging or other external applications.

On the Facebook website (www.facebook.com), you can add friends to your site and send them messages, notifying them about your book's publication. In addition, you can join networks organized by city, workplace, school, and regions. Millions of people use Facebook every day to keep their friends from all around the world updated on their lives. Another good idea would be to create and lead a Facebook group dedicated to your book's subject. You can also encourage your friends to set their status page to reading your book – alerting them in this way and inviting feedback can be an effective means of promoting your book.

One of the advantages of publishing a book is that it can also introduce you to new friends and other writers. Authonomy (www.authonomy.com) was established by HarperCollins as a community site for writers, readers and publishers to highlight new talent and provide them with a showcase for their work on the internet and receive feedback from other avid readers and writers. Authonomy.com invites you to join an online book community, champion the best new writing and build a personal profile that reflects your writing talents and opinions.

The Writewords website (www.writewords.org.uk) offers an authors' forum, with inspiration and feedback to writers, advice, interviews and articles from leading authors, as well as info. about the latest writing jobs, opportunities, competitions and news. Similarly, the Writers' News Writing Magazine (www.writersnews.co.uk) enables you to publicize the publication of your book and receive advice from other writers.

Lovewriting (www.lovewriting.com), which is linked to the UK book club Lovereading (www.lovereading.co.uk), was created to bring independently published authors and independently-minded readers closer together. It offers traditional and self-published authors access to an online customer base. Lovewriting offers advice on publishing your work, and makes it easy for people to sample, review and purchase your book.

Writing groups can also provide a useful network of friends who can review your book and help you to spread the word about its publication. The National Association of Writing Groups (www.nawg.co.uk) is a useful resource in this regard.

CHAPTER 8

Direct Marketing & Advertising

Direct marketing means sending general messages directly to potential book buyers, without the use of intervening media. This includes direct mailing and e-mailing to readers, fans, readers' groups and relevant literary organizations or businesses, and is often unsolicited. The contact that you make with these parties will be focused on a specific call-to-action, so you can track the responses from those that you approach.

The difficulty with direct marketing techniques is that everyone associates this method with the endless unsolicited printed adverts which are tucked into your letterbox every day, the spam that piles up in your e-mail inbox, or the telemarketers calling each month to sell double-glazing. Fortunately, some people today have spam filters that sift the wheat from the chaff, phone services such as which block unsolicited telephone calls, and a lucky few have dogs which can ward off people with backpacks full of printed promotional offers.

With this in mind, the question is should you engage in direct marketing for your book, or might it be counterproductive because although you might generate some interest in your book, you might upset a much larger number of people in the process, which might in turn make disparaging remarks about your book on Amazon, in other book reviews, etc.

The answer to this question is not should you do this, but what sort of direct marketing should you do which is likely to be most effective and least intrusive or offensive. To explain this more fully, I will first explain what the purpose of direct marketing for your book, and how you can best achieve those ends.

On a larger scale, direct marketing include mailing/e-mailing, dealing with responses, capturing data, data processing, and monitoring sales and marketing trends. On a smaller scale for your book, direct marketing involves the following stages:

1. Compiling an appropriate list of people or organisations to contact.
2. Tailoring your letter or e-mail to the relevant persons/organisation.
3. Deciding when would be best to send the mailing/e-mailing
4. Dealing with any replies

I will deal with each of these steps individually, explaining whom to contact, what to say and how to say it, when to contact them and how to handle any responses.

List of Contacts

Firstly, I would not recommend embarking on a massive direct marketing campaign by engaging professional marketers who promise to "contact 30,000 people in their advertising database". Often, there is no way that you can tell what they've done, and thereby no way to track whether it was worthwhile.

Similarly, there are plenty of mailing lists that you can purchase on the internet, but it is impossible to know in advance how useful, accurate and updated they will be.

What you need to do is compile your own mailing list, or find a relevant directory in the library with that information in it. This list will depend on the genre of your book and what you want recipients of your message to do. If you have written a children's book, you might want to compile a list of local and regional educators or librarians and e-mail them about your book, possibly offering to visit the school or library and read directly from your book.

If you've written a crime novel, then you might want to contact the organizers of the various crime festivals. If you've written a book, say, about suffering with depression or IVF, then you might want to compile a list of relevant organizations from the internet and raise awareness of your book by contacting them and asking them to include a link to your book in their monthly newsletters.

If you want to send a letter or e-mail to various writing circles around the UK inviting them to offer feedback on your manuscript, you can find a useful list of 120+ "Writing-Circles, Literature Courses and Workshops" listed in a Directory by the same name from www.writers-circles. com.

If you would like to raise your profile as a published author and raise awareness of your book's publication amongst publishers and agents, you can ascertain their details from

The Writer's Handbook or a fuller list of agents from the website www.firstwriters.com

If you would like for your book to be reviewed by newspapers, magazines or major UK bookclubs, you can find directories in the library with their contact details.

What to Say

What to say in your letter will depend on what you want the recipient to do, whether it be to buy your book, to review your book, to tell others about your book and mention it in their newsletters, and so on. Whatever you would like to achieve, you have to ask yourself what's in it for them, ie. why should they take time from their busy schedules or devote space in their newsletters or advertising fliers to help you promote your book?

This is why it's important to tailor your correspondence to the person that you're writing it to. Rather than saying "Dear Sir or Madam" or not even addressing anyone which is the tell-tale sign that you could care less about them and you've probably just done a simple e-shot, if you can at least address the letter or e-mail to the person, that will improve your chances considerably of receiving a positive reply.

If you are sending direct e-mails, do not send them to "undisclosed-recipients" or copy everyone and their neighbour into the e-mail to make it as easy as possible for you to send them all at once. Think about how this looks to the recipient. You are asking them to help you personally achieve something important to you, but you are asking them in an impersonal manner. The more you can address them in a personalised way, the better.

The tone of your letter really matters. You should say that you know how busy they are, but you would be grateful if they could take a look at your website, or your book, and send you feedback on it or review it. You should not hype up your book, because that will often lead to the reader being disappointed if they think, as you might be tempted to say, that it is better than *Harry Potter* or more gripping than Dan Brown's novels.

If you are writing to newspapers, magazines or literary circles inviting them to review your book, then you will need to include a printed copy of your book. They are not going to buy your book just for the privilege of reviewing it for you. If you write to them, it is always more professional if you can do so on printed letterhead devoted to your book, with an eye-catching bookmark.

When to Say It

You should wait until your book is in print for a month before approaching anyone to buy, read or review your book. The reason is because it can take a while for your book to appear for sale on Amazon and for the price to come down as book sellers like The Book Depository, EBookMole, The-Books-Warehouse sell it "New and Used" for less than the full retail price. This gives potential purchasers a wider range of choice which can make a difference in terms of book sales.

Also, it can take up to 2 - 6 weeks for your book to find its way onto the computers and eventually onto the shelves of many bookshops. One reason for this is because your book first needs to be added to the distributors' "New Publications" CD which is sent out to their bookshops and uploaded weekly in the case of larger book chains, or monthly in the case of many smaller, independent bookshops to the computer database. There is nothing worse than raising awareness of your book's publication, and then readers to ask for it at their local bookshop, only to be told "it is not listed" or "it is not available yet."

In sum, you can engage in direct marketing, but try to personalize the letters and e-mails that you send as much as you can. The more time you can spend in their regard, the more likely that it will be effective, and the more likely that you will receive positive reviews of your book, which is an essential part of book promotion, as explained in the next chapter.

CHAPTER 9

Book Reviews & Endorsements

Book Reviews

One way to generate publicity and sales for your book is to get it reviewed. But how do you go about it? The obvious answer seems to be to simply mail out copies of your book, but chances are that your potential reviewers are already inundated with books review requests.

Some publishers will work with authors to help them get book reviews, depending on the company's size and promotional budget. Some publishers will have a ready list of useful contacts who have previously reviewed their other books. Find out how many review copies your publisher is willing to provide, and whether they will do the mailing for you. With some of the larger publications, your publisher will have to request a pre-publication review.

You should target magazines, journals and websites that review books in your genre. Sending out books for review without adequate research beforehand is likely to result in your book being donated to the local library (at best), and tossed in the bin (at worst), without being read. Put together a list of companies and individuals to approach, and then send a letter or e-mail and compliment them on their reviews, asking if they would be willing to review your book. It might be a good idea to check with other authors to find out how they got reviews for their books, and if they've written books in the same genre, they may well have a list of contacts to write to in this regard.

Even if your publisher is willing to provide review copies and a list of contacts, you should also do your own research and make further enquiries. You should carefully research the reviewer's style and submission requirements. Some publications prefer requests by e-mail rather than post. Others only accept requests from publisher. Often, authors aim too high and send their book for review by publications such as the Times Literary Review, whereas it might be better to seek reviews from local and regional newspapers.

Remember, it is not just about getting reviews, it is about getting *positive* reviews, and the more thorough your research and the more professional your approach, the more likely you are to secure the sorts of reviews which will help to promote your book. There are some reviewers and websites which tend to be overly critical, and you want to make sure that you avoid sending your book to them.

Getting Reviews For Your Book

Once your book is published, you should send a tailored press release to everyone on your contact list, offering or enclosing free review copies. It is important to remember to personally thank anyone who does positively review your book, as they are much more likely to do the same for your next book, and recommend your recently published book in their literature or on their website. It is a good idea to focus on specific writers (both reviewers and feature writers) and send them a short informative letter or e-mail with a line or two about the book, mentioning that you have already read a review that they wrote ("I read with interest your write-up of *The Final Countdown* and thought you might be interested in my new crime novel entitled *Brass Knuckles*"), relevant detail about your book including the name of the publisher, ISBN number, page count, retail price, and the publication date. Most importantly, make sure that you include your contact details – not a mobile telephone number or postal address only – but an e-mail address and landline telephone number for them to contact you on. Make it as easy for them as possible to contact you and review your book.

It is important to tailor your letter or e-mail to the individual who will be undertaking the review. If the reviewer thinks that you are asking them personally to review your book, then they will be more likely to take the time to review it and disposed to write a positive review. Often, the press release you wrote for your book (as discussed in Chapter 4) can be tailored for review requests.

Checklist of details to include in your letter:

- Title of Book
- Approximate length of book
- Genre of Book
- Name of Publisher
- ISBN number
- Date of Publication
- Brief about the book (1 – 2 paragraphs)
- Brief about the author (one paragraph will due)
- Your contact details (with landline telephone & e-mail address)

Sample Letter

Dear Editor [or preferably the Editor's name, if known],

I read with interest the review that you wrote for [book title]. I am the author of a new crime novel [insert your book description]. Would you be interested in reviewing [book title] for [name of publication or website]?

I have enclosed a review copy [or I would be happy to send you a review copy upon request].

Kind regards,

[Your name]
http://www. [your website address]
Book Title
Author
Publisher
ISBN

Brief synopsis - about 25-50 words.

Further tips for favourable reviews

There are numerous ways that you can maximize the publicity from reviewers.

Firstly, encourage people on your mailing list to post customer reviews on Amazon and Barnesandnoble.com if they liked your book.

Keep an eye out for websites and publications that will agree for you to reprint their reviews on your website, because you should seek their consent before doing so as a professional courtesy. Many reviewers like to see their reviews and their names quoted elsewhere, so it is useful to extend this courtesy to them.

Join online groups where reviewers will kindly review your book and encourage you as a writer. There are plenty of review websites for every genre. Many magazines and newspapers are looking for books to review. You'll be surprised how many will take you up on the offer to review your book.

Keep a close record of everyone who responds positively and contact them again when your next book comes out.

If you self-published, *The Self Publishing Magazine* (www. selfpublishingmagazine.co.uk) is a UK print magazine offering detailed advice and case studies about self-published books. The magazine also incorporates the *Readers' Review Magazine* which publishes independent reviews of self-published books.

Other useful review sites include:

http://www.authonomy.com
http://www.oncewritten.com/About/
GettingYourBookReviewed.php
http://www.reviewthebook.com
http://www.selfpublishingreview.com

You can also try Yahoo groups. There are several where you can list your books and request reviews, such as The Reviewers Choice, the Writelist, or My Book Is Out.

For information about uploading reviews on Amazon, see:

http://www.amazon.com/gp/richpub/syltguides/fullview/
RNCWTLEMV71VM

~~~~~~~~~

Book Endorsements

Testimonials and endorsements are an important part of
your sales and marketing strategy. Whether you need an
endorsement to highlight a particular section or aspect of your
book, or you would like a testimonial to lend credibility and
excitement about your book, they can affirm your expertise
in writing about the subject matter for non-fiction books,
and affirm you prowess for fiction writing. The purpose of
endorsements is to impress your readers, and impress upon
them the message that you are intended to convey.

The time to request endorsements is before your book is
published, so that you can add a short quote from the
endorser on the back cover of your book. You also want the
opportunity to add impressive endorsements to your media
kit and press releases.

For non-fiction books, especially trade books, you should
seek endorsements from professionals or well-respected
individuals in your field which indicates that your book
provides important information and value to potential
readers. For example, if you are a life coach and you are
writing a new self-help guide, then you might ask the head
of your organization to write a short quote for you to add to
the back cover of your book.

If you have written a novel, then you might ask a well-known
author in your genre to promote your book. For example,
let us say that your book is a crime novel. You might attend

a crime festival, introduce yourself to one of the established authors in this genre and ask them if they could spend a few minutes reading the synopsis for your book and if so, if they like the premise for the book, would they mind providing a short quote for the back cover. Alternatively, you could look up established authors in your genre on the internet and send them a copy of your manuscript, asking if they would endorse it.

Aim for the stars when requesting endorsements – ask people who are recognizable in your field and who are as well known and widely known as possible. Keep in mind that granting endorsements is also of great benefit to the persons providing them, so do not be afraid to ask. Free publicity is always a bonus. When your book is published, those providing endorsements will also establish themselves further as experts or authorities within the field or genre in which you write. So, endorsements are mutually beneficial.

Be respectful of the time of the people you are approaching for endorsements. Value their hectic schedules and understand that you are not their utmost priority. Busy people may not have time to read your book from cover to cover, so do the work for them. Send them a few versions of endorsements that you would like, allowing them to choose one or top and tailor one of them. You will be surprised at how many people are happy for you to write a draft endorsement for them, for them to put their name to. Drafting sample endorsements will increase your chances of others agreeing to them and it allows you to emphasize the points you want to make to impress and impress upon your readers.

Write endorsements that are relevant to the expertise of the endorser. Writing "The best book I have read in some time" will not do. Similarly, being too detailed like "This book is about John as he grows up during the War" sounds boring. The endorsement should convey the fact that the reader will find the book interesting, informative, inspirational, etc. Your endorsements must make buyers feel good or solve a problem for them. If you are selling a healthy lifestyle book, do not write "I really liked this book". Instead, you could say "Inspirational.... it really made me feel young again" or if your novel is about the tribulations of growing up in the War Years, the endorsement might read "Charming, moving, uplifting.... it took me back to my youth."

Keep endorsements relevant and pithy, with one to two lines being sufficient. Readers don't want to read an essay about your book – you have only a few seconds to attract their attention and relay your message. Let us say that you were returning a book to the library, and the librarian asks you what you thought about the book. What would you say?

As your book sells more copies, you may receive unsolicited endorsements by way of your website from readers who liked or benefited from your book. Keep a file of them for inclusion in your promotional campaign for this book and for future books that you might write.

Even if you have already published your book, it is often worthwhile to seek celebrity or authoritative endorsements which can be added to your on-going marketing. Also, when the published does a future print run or revised edition of your book, you can add a strap line or quote to the front and back cover of your book. It is never too early or too late to seek testimonials and endorsements for your book.

Book clubs and genre-specific organisations are also a good source of endorsements for your book. If you can convince one of the main national reading groups to recommend your novel such as Lovereading or the Director of the National Literary Trust, then that endorsement will get read by thousands of book lovers. There are literary and trade organizations for most every genre of book, and you might ask them for advice and contacts in this regard.

CHAPTER 10

Social Networking

Networking is interacting with others for mutual benefit, which is integral to the sales of your book and your success as a writer. For anyone who is shy or reluctant to do so, all I would say is try it, and you'll like it. Even authors with a niche market need to network to raise awareness of their book and raise their literary profile. The more you network effectively, the more successful you and your book will be. Networking is basically telling people about you and your book one-to-one, and it is one of the most effective means of viral (word-of-mouth) marketing, or if done on the internet, word-of-mouse marketing.

Word-of-Mouth Marketing

If you want to maximize the commercial success of your book, and let others know that you're a writer, then you cannot be a shrinking violet nor keep your light under a bushel. Rather, you need to burn the shoe leather and tell people about it. Some writers will literally climb Mt. Everest to generate publicity for their book, but others can be similarly effective by joining the right literary organizations.

There are general UK organizations for writers, as well as specific associations based on genre, gender, religion, region, and so on.

In general, there is:

<u>Authors' Club</u> – Welcomes writers, agents, publishers, critics, journalists and anyone involved in literature and the written word. Administers a number of awards and organizes regular talks and dinners with well-known speakers.

<u>Authors' Licensing & Collecting Society</u> – Represents authors in terms of photocopying and lending rights for their books. The society is a main resource and leading authority on copyright matters and writers' collective interests.

<u>The Society of Authors</u> – For authors with agents only, advising them on various aspects of book publishing. There are groups within the SoA for academic writers, children's book writers, educational writers, and medical writers, as well as some regional groups. Annual subscription can be costly.

For specific *genres* of writing, there is:

<u>British Guild of Travel Writers</u>

<u>British Science Fiction Association</u>

<u>Children's Book Circle</u> – Provides a discussion forum for children's books.

<u>Circle of Wine Writers</u>

<u>Crime Writers' Association (CWA)</u>

<u>Fellowship of Authors and Artists</u> – Established in 2000 to promote and encourage the use of writing and all forms of art as a means of therapy and self healing.

<u>Garden Writers' Guild</u>

<u>The Guild of Food Writers</u>

<u>The Guild of Motoring Writers</u>

<u>Horror Writers Association</u>

<u>National Assocations of Writers in Education</u>

<u>Society of Children's Book Writers & Illustrators</u>

<u>The Romantic Novelists' Association</u>

For *women*, there is:

<u>The Society of Women's Writers & Journalists (SWWJ)</u> – Holds regular events including workshops and visits to places of literary interest. Annual Summer Festival, Autumn Lunch, and Christmas get-together feature well-known guest speakers, and biennial residential Weekend Conference features talks, discussions, and workshops on a range of topics. Also offer overseas trips of particular interest to writers.

<u>Women Writers Network (WWN)</u> – Provides a forum for the exchange of information, support, career and networking opportunities for working women writers. Meetings, seminars, excursions, newsletter and directory.

Christian writers can join:

<u>Association of Christian Writers</u> – Organizes inspirational events, effective resources and professional advice for writers who are Christians.

<u>The Arts Centre Group</u> - Brings together Christians who are working professionally in the field of the arts.

In *regional* terms, there is:

<u>Irish Writers' Union</u> – Promotes the interests and protects the rights of Irish writers

<u>Isle of Man Authors</u> – For writers living on the Isle of Man

<u>New Writing North</u> - Development agency for Northern writers

<u>New Writing South</u> - Open to all creative writers in the South East

<u>New Writing Partnership</u> - Development agency for the East of England

<u>Scottish Arts Council</u> - Championing the arts for Scotland - Europe's premier script

<u>Society of Authors in Scotland</u> – Organizes meetings, social functions and bookshop events throughout Scotland

<u>The Writing Centre</u> - For writers and writing in Cornwall and the South West

<u>West Country Writers' Association</u> – Annual newsletters, regional meetings to discuss news and views

These various organisations offer authors the opportunity to meet well-known authors and publishers, and be kept up to date on latest developments within their respective area of literary interest.

Writers often think that if they write a good enough book, a literary agent and publisher will offer to represent them and publish their book, and the agent and publisher will work together to market the book for them. However, writing a good book is only the first step in establishing yourself as a published author and reaching the market with your book. Unless a writer actively networks and is proactive in promoting their own book by raising his or her profile and building up a readership, it is unlikely that their book is ever going to achieve the recognition that it should.

Word-of-Mouse Marketing

In the digital age in which we live, national and international networking is much easier.

The internet is an amazing tool for marketing, as the world is literally at your fingertips. It is the quickest and most cost-effective way to market your book, if done correctly.

Let me begin by briefly explaining a few of the most effective social networking sites on the internet today, namely Facebook, Twitter, MySpace, Ning and Bebo.

On **Facebook**, users invite their friend to join their network and send them messages, updating their personal profiles to notify friends about themselves. It is an easy way to stay in touch with friends, and keep them informed of what is happening in your life, *such as publishing a new book*. Users can join relevant networks organized by city, workplace, school, and region. Rather than e-mailing all your friends individually to tell them about your book, you can tell them all at once this way.

To create a Facebook page of your own, go to - http://www.facebook.com/advertising

Choose the appropriate option from Local; Brand or Product; or Artist, Band, or Public Figure. You may want to choose the third and then 'writer', if you are promoting with your name. Otherwise, choose Brand or Product and then 'website' to link to your book promotion blog (more on blogging in Chapter 11). Once you are done creating your page, be a fan of it to add it to your personal Facebook profile.

Then, import your blog's feed through the 'Notes' feature on the page you just created. You can use your FriendFeed feed to post directly to your Facebook page. This will update all your social network activities to this page and keep your readers updated. You can use your FriendFeed or your blog's normal RSS feed to post on Notes.

Next, you need to build a fan base or following for the page you just created. Share your new page with your friends, and ask them to invite their friends. Make it into a viral marketing campaign, where anyone who joins invites their friends, and they in turn invite their friends, and so on.

You can a put link to your Facebook page profile on your blog, and let visitors know about your site's Facebook presence. This is important because in your Facebook page, you can add the feed to your site, along with your updates, relevant links, and anything else you want to tell others about your book. You can also share your book's Amazon link and reviews posted by any other user or website.

You can also place an advertisement on Facebook for your book which will be delivered to millions of people, where you either agree to "pay for page impressions" or "pay for clicks" to your page. The advertisement can be tailored to your website, your book's Facebook page and your blog. This will bring in a lot of visitors, but as mentioned in Chapter 2, there are problems associated with this form of pay-per-click advertising. Still, it might be worth dipping your toe in the water and spending a small amount on this form of advertising to see the sort of visitors that it brings to your book's Facebook page. You can target your audience by geographical location, age, sex, keywords, education, workplace, relationship status, relationship interest and languages through Facebook ads.

You can track your visitor activity using another Facebook application called Facebook Insights. By understanding user activity and performance, fans and ad respondents, and trends and comparisons, you will be better equipped to improve your book's adverts on Facebook and elsewhere. Facebook Insights is a free service for all Facebook pages and advertisements.

Twitter.com enables its users to send and read messages known as *tweets*. Tweets are text-based posts of up to 140 characters displayed on the author's profile page and delivered to the author's subscribers who are known as *followers*. Senders can restrict delivery to those in their circle of friends or allow open access. So, if you are on twitter, you can send your followers a tweet telling them that your new book is published, and see what they tweet back. You do not want to send to many tweets to friends about how wonderful your book is, as they may begin to think that you are a bit of a twit instead.

You can tweet others about blog entries, your book launch and upcoming speaking engagements. When promoting your book via a short 140-character pitch, include a catchy headline and a link to every blog post or review article. Do not overdo it. Not every tweet should be self-promoting. Take time to forge relationships on Twitter and familiarize yourself with how Twitter works before using it to promote your book.

If you are looking to promote your book by writing articles, fortunately many magazine and newspaper reporters are on Twitter. Read up on their articles and tweet them about your book. When you tweet an editor, you can draw attention to a query or just make small talk so they will be aware of your name when they see your query. If nothing else, get access to the reporter's personal website and hopefully their email address for future queries.

Myspace.com performs the simple act of expanding the number of people you know by meeting your friends' friends, their friends' friends and their friends' friends' friends. This is how it works in three easy steps:

1. You join MySpace and create a profile.
2. You invite your friends to join MySpace and search MySpace for your friends who are already members. These people become part of your initial "Friend Space."

3. All of the people in your friends' Friend Space become part of your network. You now have connections to more people than you did 15 minutes ago.

You can request to add anyone to your Friend Space, and if your invitation is accepted, you can send that person an e-mail, SMS messages or link to your book.

In your profile, you can write about your book, as well as your literary inspirations and aspirations. You might mention your goals as a writer, your next book project, your literary achievements and any reviews that have been written about your book. You can provide links to online websites where your books are available for purchase, including your own website or blog.

Add pictures of the front and back covers of your book. If you are going on any book tours, or having any book signings, provide dates for those as well, and make sure that you keep your Myspace profile up to date. Include contact information for those who would want to contact you for book signings and appearances.

Browse for groups that have writers or those that are authors who are promoting their own books. Add other members of those groups as friends and contact them about tips and ideas for promoting your book.

Ning.com is one of the first sites that enables you to create your own social networking site based on a particular subject. The site you create can be about anything you want it to be. Let us say that your book is based on a local legend. You can initiate your own social network of people who are interested in that particular legendary place or story.

The Web log facility on Ning is simple to use. Just click on "Create a new blog post" from your profile page and write your blog entries. Friends are easy to make on your own network because you are all there for the same reason, because they are interested in the subject matter. If you would like, you can have all the activity from the group listed on your profile so you can see what others are socializing about on Ning.

You can upload your own Youtube video (as discussed in Chapter 11) to your profile as well, as well as excerpts from your writing, copies of reviews and links to your book.

Ning also has forums and groups features. Forums are useful for getting opinions from members or telling them about upcoming events such as your book launch or book signings. Groups add depth to your social networking site. When your members create groups they are saying that they have particular interests and they want to know who else shares their interests. Then they can all talk about it on the forum.

To use Ning, you need to go to the Ning homepage (www. ning.com) click "Join Now" in the upper right which will take you to another page where you will be asked to enter your name, e-mail address, password (twice) and birthday. You need to name your new social network and to give it a website address which will end with .ning.com

Think of a descriptive, yet creative name for your new social network and type it in the name box. Then type a shortened version of that name into the web address box. Click on "Create".

On the next page you will have to choose several options for your social networking site:

1. *Privacy:* The first will be to decide whether you want to open your network to the public, or make it by invitation only.
2. *Tagline:* Give your social networking site a subtitle or add a catch phrase for your site.
3. *Describe:* Tell everyone what your social networking site is about, what they can find there and what they can expect to get out of joining it.
4. *Keywords:* These are so people can find your social networking site when they are searching for it. Use words and phrases that describe your site and words concisely and phrases that you think people would use to find it if they were doing a search.
5. *Language:* Choose a language for your site.
6. *Icon:* Every site has a picture, photo or other type of graphic to help people see what it is about and to catch people's attention. If the subject is your book, then the front cover would suit.
7. *Features:* Decide which features you need and want your members to be able to use. Drag and drop the features you want onto the page, placing them where you want them.
8. *Appearance:* Choose a theme for your social network. These come in different colours and with different designs on them. There are quite a few different themes to choose from.

You can use the advanced colour boxes to change the theme or create your own.

9. *Questions:* Choose questions you want your members to answer when they sign up for your social network. There are a few sample questions already there that you can use. Make up the rest yourself. What do you think your members will want to know about the other members? Do not be intrusive.

10. *Launch:* Once you click on the "Launch!" button your social network will be up and running. You can then invite people to join your network and submit the address of your Ning site to members of your other social networking sites inviting them to join.

Bebo.com is an acronym for "Blog Early, Blog Often". Bebo is different from other social networking sites in that it has a section dedicated to writers. In the <u>Bebo Authors</u> section of the site, also known as Bebo Books, authors can upload chapters of their books and get them reviewed. Friends' updates to Facebook, Twitter, Flickr, and other services can also be viewed, if those friends have linked those accounts to their Bebo profile.

If you click the "Authors" tab on Bebo.com, you can browse published and unpublished works either by genre or via Bebo's book charts. Visiting a book's profile will allow you to read an extract, or if you are signed into your Bebo account, you can leave comments, write a review, or add yourself as the book's "fan".

To set up a profile on Bebo for your book, click on the "Authors – Register You Book" link in the authors section of the site. If you do not have a personal Bebo profile, you will need to register for one, and if you would like, you can change the privacy settings so that your personal profile can be only seen by those you have added as friends.

Once your personal profile has been configured, you can register your book on the site, entering the title, tag line, assigning it a category and entering a 1000 word description. For published books, you can also add the publisher and the book's ISBN number.

You then have a profile which you can customize with the cover of your book (click on 'upload profile photo'). You can add an extract ('add a chapter' under the 'Read' tab), set up a blog or a poll, and pick a more appropriate design for your profile ('change skins').

Promoting your book through social networking sites eliminates geographical barriers, is more convenient, cost-effective, and records your marketing success with reviews, recommendations, and articles which will be published online for some time to come. It will not replace the benefit of getting your book into bookstores, but it enables you to tell others around the world who might be interested in reading your book once it has been published.

Participating in forums and discussion boards

Many authors participate on forums and discussions boards on various author-related websites, and include a picture of their book cover and a tagline about their book on their postings to ostensibly promote themselves and their book. These include:

ABCtales.com
Absolutewrite.com
Authorsden.com
Firstwriter.com
Sffchronicles.co.uk (for Sci-fi writers)
Writersandartists.co.uk
WritersNews.com
WriteWords.org.uk

….to name just a few.

For the most part, these sites are useful resources for authors. The difficulty, however, with some of these discussion forums, especially the ones with anonymous postings, is that they are often replete with vitriolic criticism and can be dominated and tend to serve the interests of those who moderate the discussion boards and may not be the best means to raise your profile and build up a readership for your book.

In sum, they may be useful for information, but not as useful for promoting your book. It is better to focus on social networking sites and other forms of online marketing such as Web logs, Podcasts and promotional videos, as explained in the next chapter.

CHAPTER 11

Blogging, Podcasts & YouTube

Create Your Own Blog

Another means of promoting yourself online is by upload information about yourself and your book in a web journal or diary known commonly as a weblog or "blog" for short. You can include a blog on your website, or a blog can substitute for a website and drive traffic to your site. Blogger.com, Gather.com and Wordpress.com each provide blogging tools that enable you to create a professional blog for you as an aspiring author. Once you have set up your blog, you can provide a running commentary about your book and visitors to your blog can add their own insights and comments to your posting. Be sure to update your blog regularly, which is easy to do, with fresh news, relevant information, links to any book reviews and articles, and so on.

The personal blog, which is an ongoing commentary by an individual generally arranged in chronological order, is the most common. Blogs often become more than a way to just communicate; they become a way to reflect on life as an author or works of literature. Blogging can have a sentimental quality. Few personal blogs rise to fame and the mainstream, but some blogs do garner a following such as Dr. Brooke Magnanti's diary, published initially as the anonymous blog *Belle de Jour: Diary of a London Call Girl.* Social networking sites like Twitter.com (as discussed in Chapter 11) allow bloggers to share thoughts and feelings instantaneously with friends and family and is much faster than e-mailing or writing.

A good example of well-presented personal blog is Canadian author Kate Sutherland's blog (http://katesbookblog.blogspot. com) highlighting her collection of short stories entitled *All in Together Girls.* She adds new, interesting articles to her blog every week, lists books that she is currently reading, has twitter updates, provides links to reading groups and litblogs, and has received nearly 200,000 hits to her blog in 5 years. Her blog is not overtly self-promoting, and she subtly includes an audio links to her radio interview and links to her website, publisher, MySpace Blog and retailers for her book.

Video blogging and Podcasting

Known commonly as vlogging or vidblogging, this is a form of blogging where short videos are made regularly and often combine embedded video or a video link with supporting text, images, and other metadata. Entries can be recorded in one take or cut into multiple parts. Video logs (vlogs) also often take advantage of web syndication to allow for the distribution of video over the internet as Podcasts.

In podcasting, producers record videos and make them available to anyone with a Broadband internet connection. Program listeners can then opt into a free subscription by which they receive new audio or video files that are automatically delivered either to their computers or iPods. This is an important marketing tool because you can create one by recording interviews with readers over the phone (with their consent) or by developing your own "show" in effect, showcasing your book. Your showreel or trailer will automatically be shown to the network's subscribers and delivered to their system for them to watch and listen to when they would like.

Make Your Own Youtube Video

Another very effective way to promote your book in a similar format is with a two-minute Youtube video about your book.

See, for example, William Coles' video for his book entitled The Well-Tempered Clavier - http://www.youtube.com/watch?v=F7oUrnWiZRk

Similarly, Samsun Lobe has done an excellent YouTube video for his fantasy novel Dying Star - http://www.youtube.com/watch?v=Lrn0q-elou8

This is how it is done. Firstly, you need to use a webcam or a video camera to film your video. The video for your book should not be more than a few minutes long. Keep in mind that the cheaper the camera is, the lower the quality of the video recording.

You then need to go on YouTube.com and create an account by registering on the site. Although it is possible to view most videos without an account, you do need to create an account to upload videos.

Daniel Cooke

The next step is to install the Windows Movie Maker software onto your computer. Open the program Windows Movie Maker. Go to File and start a new project. Under the file tab click "import media". Transfer your video to Windows Movie Maker. If your webcam is built into your computer, the video files may be in a public folder. Be sure to check both the public folder and the video folder.

You then need to move the video onto the "Story Board" by dragging the image of your video to the first box at the bottom of the screen. You can add transitioning effects by clicking on the effects tab in the edit section under "tasks" on the left-hand side.

Once you have done this, then add music into the Timeline by clicking on Story Board and highlighting Timeline. Import any audio that you want and drag it to its desired position in the Timeline. To move the audio around, simply drag the file. To split it into different sections, highlight the section you want split and click on the icon labelled "split" on the right side under the video preview screen. Right click on the audio file to fade it in or out. The audio levels and volume can also be adjusted accordingly.

Preview your video to make sure that it is as you want it to be. Click on the "publish movie" tab under "file". Then, sign into your YouTube account and click on My Account. Click on the new tab and highlight "video upload". Browse for your video and click "upload video". Depending on the length of your video, it can take anywhere from 5 – 10 minutes to upload and as long as an hour to process.

View your video once it is processed. Add relevant tags and keywords to generate more hits. Make sure the title and description are in your keywords. Subscribe to users and add them as friends. Commenting on others' videos is a great way to get your video channel noticed, in much the same way that reciprocal links on your website can help to achieve a higher ranking on search engines.

CHAPTER 12

Newspapers, Magazine & Radio Coverage

Once you have a professional media kit prepared and a press release drafted, about a month after your book is published you should begin to approach the printed media for articles and reviews. You should focus your initial promotional activities on local and regional media outlets, then national and international media sources. You can find out more about local media sources at your local library. Compile a list of local and regional publications and contact them directly asking whether they might be interested in receiving a press pack and possibly reviewing your book, or better still, interviewing you about your recently-published book. Do your research before contacting them. Make sure that you note down the name and if possible, e-mail address of a particular person to address your cover letter and press pack or tailor your press release to.

Not many media outlets will run a story or review your book simply because you ask them to, as they are not in the business of free advertising. You need a particular hook or angle for them to write about, such as a human interest story or a tie-in with current affairs.

Newspaper coverage

It is a waste of time to for you to approach the leading broadsheet such as the Times Literary Review, Guardian or Observer newspapers for reviews, especially for self-published books. The reviews which they do will be for traditionally published books, and the requests for these reviews are often initiated by your publisher rather than the author.

Local newspapers should be your first port of call. You should ask to speak with the newspaper's Features Editor. You may be asked what you would like to speak with them about. Tell them that you live locally, that you read their publication each week and you see they occasionally write articles featuring local authors, that you recently published a book which might be of interest and briefly explain to them why.

They may ask you whether you have a press pack or press release which you could send to the Features Editor. If so, perhaps tell them that you would like to speak to the Editor firstly if possible to see whether they might be interested in your story, and ask when would be a good time to ring them back. You will have a better chance of getting a Feature article on your book if you can speak to the Features Editor firstly to gauge their interest and tailor your press pack accordingly (as discussed in Chapter 3). Getting a feature article or review is much more effect than purchasing advertisement space, because the former is an implied endorsement and lends credibility to your book.

You can also run a competition with your local newspaper, and provide them with a few complimentary copies of your book to send to competition readers who, write in with the name of the author of the book. You should always have a half dozen books readily at hand to send for promotional purposes, as well as the contact details of the person responsible for public relations or sales and promotions at your publishing company, and ask them to send complimentary copies of your book for you for this purpose (or kindly replace the ones that you send) when a media company agrees to do an article, run a competition or do a review of your book. Most all publishers, including most reputable self-publishing companies such as Authorhouse, will send complimentary copies directly to the media source if you ask the media person to contact them directly and provide them with details for doing so. You should liaise with your publisher's PR person in advance to find out what they will do for you in this regard.

If you are invited to send in a press pack or press release for your book, leave it a few weeks after you have done so and if you have not heard back, then follow up with the Features Editor to make sure that they received the press release, but do not pester them, as they will simply ignore or delete your release if you chase them too much. Reporters who work at daily newspapers typically get stories out within a day or two, but feature writers have longer lead times, and usually start and plan work on features weeks in advance of their publication dates.

If they do agree to do an article or review of your book, make sure that they receive hi-resolution photo of you and your book cover and ask them more than once to mention your website or blog address and most importantly, where people can buy your book, including the ISBN number, and how much it will cost. All of this information should be on your press pack or press release, but you should still double-check with them on this. The more information about you and your book in the article, the better.

You might also ask whether it would be possible for you to see the article or review before it is published. You need to be really tactful when making this request, possibly emphasizing that you are not interested in editing the article or review in any way, but that you want to make sure that the details are all correct. In the case of a review, this will also help to ensure that it is a positive review. Even if they say "it is not their policy to do this" and do not grant your request, the fact that you have asked to see the article or review prior to publication usually puts them on notice that you really care about what they have to say about your book.

Retain copies of any newspaper articles or reviews, scanning them in at a high resolution and saving them as jpeg or tiff files, and upload them to your website or blog. If you do not have a scanner or do not know how to do this, then your local printer should be able to do this for you for a few pounds. Alternatively, you can ask the newspaper to e-mail you a copy of the article if possible, in which case it will already be formatted digitally for you.

Make sure that you send copies of any articles or favourable reviews to your publisher, as they may want to add them to the listing of your book on their website, add a quote from the article or review to their own press pack on your book, add a strap line from the review to the front or back cover of your book for subsequent print runs, and so on. Also, they will be pleased to hear that you are actively promoting your own book, and complementing their own marketing activities. If you would like to write more books with the same publisher, then it might be a good idea to copy the commissioning editor into your e-mail to the PR person as well. The more you can show them that you are keen to promote your own book, the more disposed the editor will be to work with you on another book, and as anyone who has tried to get a book traditionally published knows that every little detail matters, and every little bit helps.

It is always a good idea to keep on the good side of your publisher, especially the commissioning editor and the sales and marketing or PR person. The more they like working with you, the more you will achieve together. All too often, authors feel that they are doing all of the promotion for their book, and not receiving the support and guidance that they would like from their publisher. However, when you complain to your commissioning editor that their sales and marketing team are not doing enough in your view, it is nearly always counterproductive. They will often come to the defence of their marketing team, and it may undermine your relationship with the people who can help you the most.

The best thing to do is ask them what their plans are in terms of marketing your book and possibly selling the foreign rights to your book, and then ask them what you can do to complement their efforts. It does no good to say to them "why haven't you done this" as it can put them on them on the defensive. Some authors think that it is the squeaky gate that gets oiled, ie. that the more they chase the publisher's sales and marketing person, the more that they will "push" their book. However, in publishing, it is often the squeaky gate that gets replaced. You might see some short-term benefit, but in the long-term, it is probably not worth it.

Rather, if you tactfully ask the marketing person at the outset what their plans are for promoting your book and for perhaps selling the foreign rights to your book, and then agree with them what more you can do to help, you should simply focus on fulfilling your own marketing commitments and keeping them (and the commissioning editor) periodically informed of your progress in this regard. It is not that you are doing their work for them, but that you are showing them that you are prepared to do your part to make your book commercially successful, and you will often find that the more you do, the more they will be willing to work with you to promote your book further and work with you on your next book.

If you have self-published your book, it is important to keep your publisher informed of any positive articles or reviews about your book, and to send or preferably e-mail press clippings or links of various online review articles to them, asking if there is any way that they can highlight these on your book's website listing, or better still, highlight them in the press section of their website or mention them in their monthly newsletters. Self-publishing companies like to promote the fact that their authors' books are in the press, as it helps them to procure more business. As it is mutually beneficial, you should take advantage of this.

Magazine promotion

Magazines, especially trade magazines, are useful for publicizing your book because they target specific audience. Consequently, magazine space is hard to come by, and the books that they mention are often in the context of a specific topic or feature article. In deciding which magazines to approach, you need to research the market carefully to make sure that firstly, they are relevant to your book's content. Let us say that you have written a novel called *Sour Grapes* which is about a conspiracy to sell high quality wines, the contents of which have been mixed with cheaper wines. Rather than approaching national weekly magazines which rarely publicize books, or tend to do so once the book has *already* garnered national recognition, it would be much more practical to approach upmarket wine-related publications such as *Decanter* and *The World of Fine Wine*, and online wine magazines and forums such as Let's Talk Wine (www. letstalkwine.com), Thirty Fifty (www.thirtyfifty.com), Love That Wine (www.lovethatwine.co.uk), Wine Pages (www. wine-pages.com) and Wine Anorak (www.wineanorak. com).

Lifestyle books often find their way into magazines. For example, let us say that you wrote a coming-of-age book called *A Small Town Life* about growing up in the country, moving to the big city, and then moving back to where you grew up with your children. There are magazines like *Town and Country, Country Living, Country Life, Country and Coast Living* and many others which might be interested in doing a feature article or review of your book. It the publishers of these magazines who think that a feel-good book about the virtues and charm of bringing up your children up in the country is going to help sell the products and services for the companies that advertise in their magazine, then they might even feature your book.

If you call magazines to make an enquiry about possibly featuring or reviewing your book, they will often pass you on to a PR and advertising colleague who will ask whether you might be interested in paying for a quarter, half or full-page advertisement for your book, and in return, they will offer you a feature article. For example, Welsh writer Mark Jones, the author of *The Crooked Cross Collection* which he self-published, paid a few hundred pounds for an excellent full-page editorial/review and half-page advertisement in *Country and Coast Magazine*, which is prominently displayed in many Debenhams stores, Venue Cymru and top Welsh hotels, as well as shops and businesses throughout the region.

The trade press is especially useful for non-fiction works written with a specific target market or profession in mind. Trade journals and trade magazines typically contain feature articles and advertising content focused on their particular industry with little if any general advertising. If your book is called *Protect Your Children From the Internet* and helps parents to avoid the dangers their children face when they surf the internet, there are literally dozens of internet trade publications such as *.net, Webuser, PC Magazine, Computeractive, PC Pro, PC Answers, Computer Shopper, PC Advisor* to name but a few which may well publish a feature article and review of your book.

The important point to remember is you should target those publications which are going to raise your profile *and* help to sell copies of your book. Any magazine will offer you advertising space for a price. But if the advertisement is not going to bring you a return on your investment in terms of actual book sales, then you might as well not do any advertising at all. For example, I know one author who took the *time out* to spend £750 for a quarter page advertisement, which generated a grand total of 3 sales for his novel. Granted this publication had a bi-annual circulation of around 80,000 readers, but if only 3 of those actually bought the book, surely his £750 investment could have been better spent, unless you are independently wealthy and you just want to see your name in a particular magazine to show your friends. Ironically, this person published his book under a pen-name, so it was a case of choosing a well-circulated, but inapposite publication to pay for promoting his book, which can be a costly mistake to make.

There are two useful magazines which often review self-published books.

The Self Publishing Magazine is a UK-based print magazine published three times a year (in April, July and October) with helpful advice for anyone who has or is planning to self-publish their own book.

Each issue contains:

- Marketing and promotional ideas for self-publishing authors.
- Tips and hints on the printing and publishing processes.
- Case studies, reviews of self-published books and the latest self-publishing news.

With expert advice on all stages of the self-publishing process from book production to pricing, printing and promotion, this magazine incorporates *Readers' Review Magazine*, which is the only UK magazine to publish independent reviews of self-published books.

Information on the current issue, back issues, a free article library, reviews and much more can be found by navigating the website (www.selfpublishingmagazine.co.uk).

The Self-Publishing Review is an online magazine to self-publishing news and reviews. It is also a social network where writers, readers, and publishers can join and connect. The aims of the site is to improve the attitude toward self-publishing and raise the profile of authors and help them to build up a readership for their writing through book reviews, publisher reviews, interviews, news and current events, feedback and advice.

You can either contact SPR asking them to review your book (which they will do for a nominal fee), or contact other members on the site asking them to review your book. SPR aims to have as many self-published books reviewed as possible. You can also post your own book reviews of self-published books by posting blog entries to the site. Once you have joined the site, added some information to your profile and are logged in, go to "My Blogs" on the navigation bar at the top and select "Self-Publishing Review", then "New Post" in the drop down menu and start blogging.

Radio interviews

Radio interviews can be easier to secure than you may think, especially if your book has a self-help, how-to, humorous, educational, social, political, travel or local interest angle. If your book is controversial for any reason, then radio interviews can provide you with the perfect opportunity to "plug" your book. As always, do your research before contacting radio stations. Go to your local library or search the internet and list the top five radio stations for you to contact. You should know or familiarize yourself with the station's programs and listener profile, and tailor your approach to suit their audience.

As with your marketing plan in general, start with local radio and work your way up to regional radio stations. If your book starts to sell well and you are well-recognized as an expert in the particular field in which you write, you can approach national radio stations. The benefit of local radio is it will enable you to practice and improve your pitch. The more radio interviews you do, the more you will know which questions to expect and be comfortable talking about your book. It is best to script any interview, to know what questions the interviewer is likely to ask you in advance so that you can prepare your responses and avoid the interviewing taking you off-track where you end up talking about matters unrelated to your book. Make sure that you mention any upcoming book events, speaking engagements or book signings and the respective dates for them.

Preparation is the key. Listen to other interviews conducted by that particular radio station to familiarize yourself with the interview format, the type of questions they are likely to ask, and the length of time devoted to responses. Understand which issues are likely to arise in relation to your book, and which responses are likely to resonate or evoke a response from their listeners. Practice answering those questions by taping your replies and listening to them back. Enlist the help of a well-meaning friend or loved one to give you constructive feedback on your responses. You might even have them do a mock interview, and encourage them to try taking you off-track so that you can practice bringing them back to the topic at hand, which is your book.

Radio interviews are generally planned in advance, and can either be held in the radio station recording studio or over the phone. If it is the latter, be sure that you take the call in a quiet place, without the possible distractions of children crying, dogs barking, trains whizzing or police cars wailing by, or mobile phones going off in the background. Try to arrange the interview at a time when the postman or pizza delivery person is not likely to arrive. Also, if it is a phone interview, it is probably a bad idea to have someone else in the room with you whilst the interview is taking place, as you need to keep fully focused on the task at hand. Unnecessary distractions and interruptions can usually be avoided with some forethought.

Take your time. There's no need to rush. Keep some notes next to you about the points that you want to make so that you can return to them if need be. Do not worry about their being "dead air" as the interviewer will keep you talking. What you need to be mindful of is that firstly, you do not over-answer questions with long-winded replies, and definitely do not exaggerate or hype your book with statements like "I really think it will be the next best-seller" or "everyone who has read it has loved it, and told me they cannot wait for the sequel". This may be true, but if I had a penny for every author who told me that they think their book "is the next big thing", I would be very rich indeed.

Secondly, do not let the interviewer side-track you about unrelated matters. Answer questions honestly and in a way that presents you and your book in the most positive and interesting light for the radio station's listeners. Do not let the interviewer lead you down a path that you do not want to go, and do not say anything to the interviewer on-air or off-air that you do not want broadcast to the public. Even if the interviewer assures you that their question and your reply will be "off the record", it will not be. Whatever you say is always "on the record". So think and plan carefully before replying.

Radio interviews tend to fly by. It will be over before you really begin to get your stride. That is why you need to hit the ground running, much like the opening few lines and pages of your book. If you feel yourself getting flustered, take a deep breath, smile (it is on the radio, after all), and give yourself a few seconds to think and compose yourself. If you are asked a question which you do not know the answer to, say that you do not know the answer rather than making believe that you do.

Again, the more interviews that you do, the more confident you will be. Make sure that you thank the interviewer and radio station for interviewing you, and invite them to contact you if there is any related matter that they would like to interview you about in future.

Lastly, remember to make a tape of your interview when it is broadcast, and upload it to your website and web log. Do not rely on the radio station to provide you with one, but if you do forget to tape it, or the sound on your taping is poor quality, you can always ask them if the station could kindly send you a copy of the interview or if you could download it as a Podcast, although there may be a nominal charge for the privilege of hearing the sound of your own voice again.

CHAPTER 13

Getting Your Book into
Bookshops & Beyond

In terms of seeing your book on bookshelves at major retail bookshops, there is a big disparity between traditionally published and self-published books, largely based on a conventional publishing model and an outdated perception of self-published books.

In brief, most traditional publishers estimate how many copies of a given book are likely to sell, do an initial print run of a few thousand books, store them in their warehouse, and work with wholesalers to distribute them to retail book and supermarket chains. They then hype books written by well-known authors, often with media tie-ins, or ghost-written celebrity autobiographies, to increase demand and get them "front of house" in bookshops. Because they will agree to stock thousands of copies at a time, major retail chains will ask publishers to discount their books to increase their margins, which makes them even more competitive.

On this model, publishers *present* books to distributors and retailers before they are even printed, and sometimes before the books are even finished. When calling on distributors or book buyers, sales reps will show them a catalogue of upcoming titles scheduled to be published in the coming months. Buyers will then use the catalogue as a reference to decide which book to buy-in initially.

The main deciding factors for them in this regard are (1) the author's track record for previous book sales (especially the author's last book, sourced from Nielsen Book Data), (2) the author's platform which is the promotional prospects which the author brings to the table. For example, is there a media tie-in, does the author have a loyal fanbase or existing readership, will the author actively promote his or her book, does the author have an website and blog, will they sell copies of their book in their own professional capacity as an educator, self-help guru, comedienne, etc., (3) the quality of the content, (4) the publisher's sales and marketing plans for the book, and (5) the cover design and any back cover endorsements.

Book distributors and retailers add up all of these factors, and then decide how many books to order based on their projected demand. Retailers then place them on their bookshelves, and if they sell well, they will then order more. The better they think the book will sell and the larger the discount from the publisher, the more likely they are to be placed front-on-shop or showcased in the bookshops' window displays, which in turn increases their commercial success. That is the traditional bookstore stocking model.

Barriers to Self-Published Books

The barriers to self-published books are much higher in terms of the prospects for getting them into bookshops. In the case of some retailers, they are insurmountable because of bygone stigmas attached to self-published books.

Firstly, there is the mistaken, but commonly-led assumption that since the book is not traditionally published, it is probably not be good enough for publication. Anyone who knows the publishing industry knows that publishers' decisions about which books to publish are often based on name recognition more than the merits of the manuscript itself, and thus the hurdles to first-time authors are higher than The Chair and more difficult to surmount than Bechers Brook. Moreover, reading some of the books on the shelves today, there is no obvious correlation between best-selling celebrity bios and Booker Prize winners.

Secondly, retailers prefer to stock books from traditional publishers because they know the book has been professionally edited that way. Retailer cannot risk their reputation by selling unedited or poorly edited manuscripts as new, because readers will complain if they purchase a book which is replete with grammatical mistakes.

Thirdly, major advances in digital and laser print technology over the last decade have led to a printing revolution in which many self-publishing and smaller publishers are turning from the traditional printing techniques (called *offset printing*) to *print-on-demand* (POD) printers like Lightning Source in the UK to fulfil books orders for them. With traditional printing, plates bearing the book's page images are prepared, and the set-up costs are the same irrespective of how many books are printed. Traditional publishers will print as many books as they reasonably can in the initial print run to keep their costs per book to a minimum and thereby offset the cost of offset printing.

With print-on demand publishing, books are saved in PDF format and printed off a computer. Thus, they can be readily printed one at a time, once they have been ordered and paid for. The benefits to smaller presses and self-publishers with there being no minimum print requirement are numerous. Whereas books are paid for in advance, there is no cashflow problem, there is no need to rent out warehouse space to stock printed books, amendments to the manuscript can readily be made, and books do not have a limited shelf life and go out-of-print once all the printed copies have been sold.

The downside to print-on-demand publishing is that the cost per copy is determined by size of the manuscript in PDF format, *ie.* by the number of pages that need to be printed. The retail price for self-published colour books, in particular children's picture books, is cost prohibitive. And if your novel is lengthy, this can make the price of your book less competitive. With regard to getting your book into bookshops, this is complicated by the fact that most retail outlets work with traditional publishers on a quantity basis, and can ask for book prices to be discounted and pass that discount onto their customers. Consequently, your self-published book which turns out to be 250 pages long in PDF format may have a fixed retail price of £10.99, whereas the same book by a traditional publisher may have a recommended retail price of £8.99 and is further discounted to £6.99 or sold at a reduced price as part of a two-book offer by the publisher and retailer to encourage more sales. These discounts are possible because of the sheer number of books that the retailer is likely to sell, and there is no such mass-market incentive with books published print-on-demand.

Finally, there is the pressing issue of "sale or return." Most traditional publishers agree with retailers that if the book does not sell after, say, 90 days, then they can return them to the publisher and their money will be refunded. This mitigates the commercial risk for retailers and enables them to place larger book orders if they feel there is a likely demand for the book. However, self-published books do not come with this money-back guarantee from the publisher even if you can convince retailers to stock your book, and thus the responsibility lies with the author to underwrite the cost of his books. In other words, the only way to get your books into many bookshops is to tell them if they order a certain number of copies for an agreed period of time, you will buy back any unsold copies after that period. Alternatively, you could buy a number of copies yourself, preferably at a special "author rate" from your publisher, and offer to supply them directly to the publisher. However, it is often independent bookshop only which will make special arrangements and concessions in this regard.

So, if you are planning to approach bookshops to see if they will agree to place your self-published book on their bookshelves, the main issues that you may need to address are:

- Because your book is self-published, it may not be very good
- Your book may have grammatical mistakes and require proof-reading
- Print-on-demand books tend to be overpriced and cost prohibitive
- They may be stuck with your book if it does not sell

With these concerns in mind, you should prepare your replies before you speak to the person responsible for deciding whether to sell your book in their bookshop, and pre-empt them if you can.

Breaking Down Bookshop Barriers

To increase the likelihood that bookshops will stock your book and display it for sale on their shelves, you need to know when to approach bookshops, whom to speak with in the store and which bookstores to approach first.

The optimal time to begin approaching bookshops is at least a *full month* after your book has been published. The reason for this, as explained in Chapter 3, is because when a book is published, most publishers will send your book's details to their distributors, who will then upload the information to their "new publications" CD and send it out to retailers. The bookshops then upload this information to their computers. This can take anywhere from 1 – 4 weeks post-publication. You do not want to traipse around various bookshops with your press packs in tow only to hear that your book is not yet listed for sale on their computers, because until it is, they will not be able to order your book in. If, after a month's time, you find that your book is still not available to purchase over the counter at major book retailers, then you should notify your publisher and ask them to check on this for you.

It is important to know whom best to speak with in the bookshops about selling your book. When you go to the bookstore, make sure you have two press packs and two copies of your book in your carry bag. Approach the person responsible for helping customers locate books within the shop, tell them that you published a book, give them the title of your book and your name and ask whether your book is currently available for sale within the shop.

They will most likely look up your book on their computer by the title or author name, or ask you for the book's ISBN number, to find out who the publisher is and to see whether it is in currently in on the shelves or in stock and available for them to order. This is why it is important to have an ISBN number for your book, as bookshops will need this number to order your book and keep track of it in their sales and marketing inventory.

Alternatively, if you see someone stocking books on the shelves, you might tell them that you have published a book and ask them who you might speak with about possibly selling your book in their bookshop. Remember that the people behind the tills are responsible for ringing up sales, and therefore may not have the time to give you all of the details that you require.

You will certainly not be the first author who has made this sort of enquiry. In fact, depending on the size of the bookstore, they probably receive dozens of requests to stock authors' own books every month. Thus, they will have a ready response for you when you ask them to sell your book, especially the larger bookshops. In terms of details you should enquire about, make sure that you have a blank piece of paper in hand to note down the person's name responsible for deciding which books are sold in the shop, and follow up with him or her after your initial query.

They might say all their books are decided by their distributor or they do not stock self-published books. For example, let us say that the person at your local Waterstone's whom you speak with says "Gardners, our wholesaler, decides which books we stock." In general, this may be the case, but exceptions can and will be made if you can speak to the store's manager or book buyer and explain why your book will appeal to their customers. Basically, you need to convince them that your book will sell, and that you will do everything you can to make sure that it does.

To answer concerns that they might have, especially with regard to those mentioned above, you can:

- Inform them if your book has been professionally or properly edited.
- Invite them to read a complimentary copy of your book so they can see that the book is interesting and well-written.
- Say you will work with them on an appropriate discount and sales commission.
- Tell them that if they order, say, a half dozen copies of your book, you will buy back any copies which do not sell within 90 days, that you would be prepared to work with them on a "sale or return" basis to get the ball rolling.

Small, independent bookshops are generally the best place to start canvassing, as their managers are often glad to sell local authors' books, whether traditionally published or self-published, and many will actually have a section of their store devoted to local authors or may agree to display your book in their shop window. You can find a useful directory of independent bookshops at this website - www. localbookshops.co.uk

Once your book is on their bookshelves, the onus is on you to make sure that your friends and colleagues go to the store and buy as many copies of your books as possible, not all at once, but every so often to encourage the bookstore owner to continue to stock, sell and possibly showcase your work. The benefit by starting with the smaller bookstores is that they are likely to say "yes", they will help promote your book for you, and you can practice your retail pitch to them. This will build your confidence, so that you are not dispirited if some of the larger book chains say "no". Success breeds success.

Carefully and subtly monitor the sales of your book in your local bookshops, if you can. Make sure that it is prominently displayed, ask the person behind the desk responsible for informing customers about book placement within the store how many copies have sold and how many they have in stock. If they have sold half of their stock, ask if they will order more copies in. If they have not sold and you may have to buy them back, then offer to do a book signing at the store to ensure that they do sell.

CHAPTER 14

Arranging Book Signings

One of the best ways to raise your profile as a published author and sell more copies of your book is by making personal appearances and book signings give you the perfect opportunity to do this. By speaking directly to potential readers of your book, you will be pleasantly surprised by the positive reception and support that bookstore browsers will offer you. Once again, the best place to start your book signing tour is with small, independent bookshops close to home. For book signings to be successful, however, requires careful planning.

When you ask bookshop managers whether they will stock your book, this might be a good opportunity for you to offer to do a book signing as well. Before you set a date, check at the local library and read the local papers to find out what other events are planned for that time to make sure that your book signing does not clash with them, or better still, to see if you can dovetail your book signing in with a local festival or busy shopping period.

Visit the bookshop again well in advance of the event to get a better feel for the space and decide what sort of presentation might work best. Ask to talk to the events co-ordinator about arrangements on the day. How many books will they be stocking for you to sign and how many should you bring with you to sell? Where will you be sitting, and what time do they expect you to arrive and leave? Will you need to bring your own table and chair? What will they be doing, if anything, to publicize your book signing? Ask the store whether they could mention your book signing event in their newsletter or other promotional mailing.

Generally, it is left to the author to arrange for a notice to be put in the local newspaper, and try to piggyback off this by asking if they would like to publish an interview with you about your book, or if they might be able to send someone to cover the event. Also, make sure that notices are put up in the shop window a few days beforehand, posters put up in your local schools and libraries with their permission, and flyers handed out on the day by friends or family outside the venue. If you can ask them to take a few photos of you during the event, you can add these photos to your website and to your press pact. Make sure the people you know are aware of the event, and ask them to come along and bring a friend.

If this is your first book, your readers probably have not met you before, and therefore the book signing is the first time they will see you except for your picture on the back cover. Dress up and wear comfortable but stylish clothing that reflects your personality and that of your writing. If your book is a children's book, you might want to dress up as one of the characters, or if you have written a book about a historical figure, you might come dressed in a period costume. It depends on whether you are comfortable or feel you need props of this kind as they can make your book signing more memorable and enjoyable, but do not overdo it, and check with the bookshop beforehand to make sure that they are okay for you to do this. If you have written a children's story like *Charlotte's Web*, it is probably not such a good idea.

Bring along a half dozen press packs for your book in case anyone associated with literary reviews or the media requests them. Bring a generous supply of bookmarks and a few free promotional gifts to hand out. You should not pass out your personal details to anyone who asks for them. Rather, take their details or business card and tell them that you will follow up with them.

While the bookstore will supply you with pens, it is possible that you will be signing a lot of books. Bring along your favourite fountain or ballpoint pen for you to sign books with, preferably one with a comfortable grip so that your hand does not give out halfway through the event, and a fine tipped pen to ensure that your signature looks professional rather than smudged. In fact, it's a good idea to have a few pens readily at hand because occasionally, your favourite pen can go missing at book signings.

What Should You Say When Signing Your Book

Work out in advance what you plan to say when signing a copy of your book. If you do not know the person, you should ask them who you should address it to, and then the minimum you should say is "To [their first name], hope you enjoy the book! With best wishes, [your first name]." You might also add the city and date below your signature, as that makes it even more personal and special for the reader. Alternatively, if there is no queue forming around the corner, you should ask the reader if there is anything in particular that they would like you to say. For example, if you are signing the book for one of their children, they might ask you to address the book specifically to them. You might be expected to say something more in keeping with the genre of your book.

If it is a humour book, you might add a short, funny line or smiley face. Depending on how busy you are, it is always good to take a minute or two to speak with your reader or fan, as they have paid you twice – they paid you a compliment by asking you to sign the book, and they actually paid for the book that you are signing for them. Thanking them for coming also goes a long way. This may be the only chance that they will have to put a face to your writing, and you want it to be memorable for them in a positive way.

Arrive early for the book signing, and enjoy a cup of coffee or tea before the limelight falls on you. If you are selling some copies of your book yourself, make sure that you have a cash float to make change. Put a bookmark in each copy that you sell on the day, as this will help promote your book after the event. Leave any extra bookmarks that you brought at the front desk, asking them to leave them out at the till to help promote your book further.

Do not be discouraged if you have not drawn much of a crowd. Do not sit behind the table and look bored or preoccupied. Circulate the room and introduce yourself to people browsing books in your book's genre. But try not to be out of sight of your book signing table, as you want to be available to fulfil any requests from book browsers to sign your book. Once the event is over, make sure that your area is clean and in the same working order that you found it. With the remaining copies of your book, ask if you can leave some signed copies with the store for them to sell in the days to come, and leave your details for them to contact you there any more interest or enquiries should arise after the event.

All of the preparation is to ensure that you enjoy the day. Before leaving, personally thank the manager of the shop and those who helped you organize and set up the event for their time and effort. Make sure you have noted down their names, and a follow-up "thank you" note never goes amiss. You may want to do a book signing there for your next book, and the better the relationship you build with the bookstore's manager and staff, the more likely they will be to welcome you back.

Organizing a Book Tour

You should do as many book signings as you can muster. Once you have exhausted local shops, you might organize more location-specific book signings. If your story takes place in a specific town or village, you might speak with bookshops in that locale about doing a book signing. William Coles, author of *The Well-Tempered Clavier*, organized a series of book signings from Edinburgh to Eton College, where his story takes place. If you can co-ordinate your book signing tour with various radio interviews, speaking engagements, and other book-related events such as a literary festival or trade fair, thereby enabling you to promote your book as much as you can while you are "on the road" so to speak, then all the better.

CHAPTER 15

Schools & Libraries

Depending on the genre and intended readership for your book, there may well be other retail outlets for your book, including schools and public libraries.

Selling Your Books to Schools

The children's book market is one of the most competitive and saturated markets to break into, especially children's picture books. If you have published a children's book, there is a ready-made market for your book, namely your local schools and libraries. Teachers often welcome visitors to read children's books to their classes, and they will have funds allocated in the school budget for purchasing copies if there is a demand for them. You have to create that demand amongst children at the school by firstly offering to read your story or excerpts from your book to them. Many authors write books based on stories which they made up to read to their children or grandchildren, so they will be confident reading the same books to children of the same age.

You can get a list of regional schools from your library. Alternatively, you can go to www.upmystreet.com and put "schools" and "[your town]" into the search facility and it will bring up schools in your area, or simply put "schools in [your town]" into Google and it will bring up various sources on the internet for this information. If you plan to do a few readings at your local schools only due to time and travel constraints, then it would probably be best to actually go to the school in advance and ask reception if you could speak with the teachers responsible for the target age group of your book about the prospect of coming in to read your book to them. You should bring a press pack with you, and leave it with the receptionist or preferably the teachers themselves, along with a copy of your book for them to peruse.

If you can agree a date and time for you to do the reading then and there, all the better. If not, check back with the teachers or receptionist in a fortnight's time if you have not heard anything further by then. This will give the teachers ample time to read your children's story and see if you can agree a suitable date for you to read to their class. If it goes well, and school readings generally do, you can build on this by organizing a competition whereby the children can draw a picture of the main character in the book, and offer to read a sequel the story or another children's book if you have written one.

If you would like to do readings from your book at various schools in your region, you might send a letter and copy of your book to the schools in advance offering to come in and read from your book, to talk about what it is like to write books, or to talk about the background or places in which the story takes place. Roland Bond, a retired school head teacher and author of *The Balaclava Brigade,* wrote to dozens of schools in and around Solihull in the West Midlands, and spoke to literally hundreds of children aged 8 – 12 year about his own life as a young evacuee from a northern Birmingham suburb to a small Midland mining village where he made friends with a group of local children. Several of the brigade's hare-brained, hair-raising and humorous exploits in this story are loosely based on his own wartime childhood experiences, which the children whom he spoke to found fascinating. Roland's stories were so well-received and the children kept asking what happened next to 10 year-old Tommy Dennis and other members of the brigade, which inspired Roland to write and publish a sequel called *The Balaclava Brigade Victorious*.

Besides raising your profile as a published author, and the sense of fulfilment that you feel when you see children enjoying and asking questions about your story, you should use this opportunity to sell the school a number of copies of your book. Roland sold over 500 copies of his books just to schools in the West Midlands. You can do this in three ways. Firstly, after you have spoken or read to a classroom of children, ask the teacher whether they would be interested in buying a dozen or half dozen copies of your book, and bring a dozen with you so that if they say "yes", you can leave them with the teacher and invoice the school within the week. If the teacher says that he or she will think about it, or that they need to talk to the head teacher firstly, then ask them when would be a good time to check back with them on this, and then do it. If, as in many larger schools, there is more than one class for children in your target age group, then you might pre-arrange to do talks to both classes on the same day.

You should ask to speak with the school librarian as well, and when you do, tell her that you just did a classroom reading, and the children were asking where they can get copies of your book to read, and you wanted to pass on those details to the librarian so they could possible order in a few copies for children to read and enjoy in their own time in the library, or at home if they are able to take the books out of the library.

Thirdly, if you time it right, there are pre-term publications which list and advertise new children's books for educators to purchase. When Welsh author Mark Jones published his children's story *Molly and Martin's Magic Computer*, he paid to advertise his book in a publication from Scholastic which lists new and exciting children's stories which was released to thousands of schools across the UK, with a link to his own website for any interested to buy his book via the online transaction provider Paypal. Mark has a few hundred copies of his book print the traditional way, and fulfilled any orders himself and sold over 700 copies of his book generating a few thousand pounds in net revenue just from this one advertisement.

To increase your exposure and sales, you can also approach major UK Book Clubs like Love Reading which has an excellent website (http://www.lovereading4schools.co.uk/) which is specifically dedicated to recommended reading for children and young adults according to their ages and reading level. If you can write to these Book Clubs and ask them whether they could read and recommend your children's story, when they agree to do so, their recommendation will reach thousands of teachers, parents and children.

Other child-related and child-friendly organisations like nurseries and nanny agencies can be useful sources for selling and marketing your book. There are children's retail shops, toy shops, early learning centres, and so on which you could also speak to about possibly placing your book for sale in the shelves in their shop. If you do not ask, then you will never know.

Often, authors think that if they can link their book to a respected charity, offering to donate something to the cause, this will help to promote their book because the charity may mention your book in their publications and newsletters, and having them endorse your book will surely enhance sales. Yet, charities are approached all of the time with people asking them to endorse their work in exchange for a donation or share in the royalties. Most charities, especially national charities, will simply say that they would just be interested in receiving a donation from you, and they do not engage in quid pro quo or royalty-based arrangements. The ones which do agree for you to mention their charity in association with your book will ask you to commit to a minimum donation to their charity, often payable in advance. They can be very guarded and inflexible about the wording on your book, the placement of their logo, and so on. It can be frustrating seeking charity-based endorsement and my advice would be to donate generously, but do not see it as a means to advertise your book or lend credibility to your writing.

Getting Libraries to Stock Your Book

You can probably get your book into your local library by walking in, asking to speak to the Head Librarian, explaining that you live locally, that you have published a book (show or give them a copy), and you would be grateful for their advice on who they could speak with to get it ordered into the library. Most will be receptive to this, and organize this for you or tell you how to go about doing so. They may tell you to speak with the central library, and give you the name of the person responsible for deciding which books are stocked in all of the municipal libraries within the area.

In fact, you should ask for the name of the person to speak with at their central library anyway because it would be better to speak with one person and have a number of copies of your book ordered for numerous libraries all at the same time. Again, it is a good idea to have a copy of your press pack and a copy of your book to show them, but there is no need for you to give them a complimentary copy, as they will have money allocated by the town or local council for buying new books for their readers.

When you speak to the Head Librarian, you might ask whether you could do a series of talks at their libraries. As with bookshops, their main incentive for you doing so would be if they felt it would bring in more members of the public to browse their shelves and use their facilities. Therefore, your talk would need to be interesting and entertaining, and have to be more than a public advertisement for your book. Your talk will need to have wider appeal. You might talk about "How to Write a Good Book", or "How to Get a Book Published." Or, you might talk about "The Right Books for Your Children to Read" which has a more public service angle to it. Some authors prefer to give talks with a more contemporary or controversial hook to it, like "Should Books be Censored?" or the more incendiary title "Should Books be Burned?" However, let the content of your book determine the title of your talk, because controversial talks can lead to provocation. You want to have a good idea of your likely audience, and for everyone who attends to feel comfortable and welcome.

The more public speaking engagement that you do, the more people will hear about you and possibly buy your book, especially if they know that you are a local author. If there are local and recognizable town landmarks mentioned in your writing, then regular visitors to the library may well take a keener interest. People generally attend talks at libraries because they feel that you might have something important and informative to say, something that will inspire or help them in some way. The more you can convey the practical aspect in the title of your talk, the more likely you are to capture their attention.

When it comes to generating public interest in your talk, some libraries will be more helpful than others in lending a hand. You need to take the initiative at every step, and ask them if you could put up posters advertising the talk around the library well in advance, ask if they can mention your talk to people who they think might be interest in attending, prepare flyers for the event and ask to leave them on the information table or where people check-out books, talk to you local council about helping to promote your talk by mentioning in their weekly or monthly newsletter of local events, and invite your family and friends to come along and ask them for feedback afterwards on how they thought it went.

You will need to make any set-up arrangements. Do you need a table to showcase your book? Will you need to arrange chairs for attendees? Once again, do not forget your favourite pen and extra pens for any books that you are asked to sign. In this regard, you might arrange for the local bookshop to supply copies of your book to sell. This will serve a dual purpose. It will help take some of the workload off your shoulders, and it may encourage the store to order and stock more copies of your book. If they see that you are actively promoting your book, then they feel more confident that your book will sell. Also, do not forget to tell them that you will mention to attendees that they can buy more copies of your book from their local bookshop.

Your talk should not be too long. Twenty minutes would suffice. Invite any questions, and it is always a good idea to offer free drinks and complimentary snacks. Thank everyone for coming, and tell them that if they have any questions for you later, they can let the librarian know and it will be passed on to you.

Make sure you thank the librarian and their staff for helping you with your talk. Ask to leave more bookmarks on their main desk, and if it goes well, which it surely will, then speak with them about possibly organising another talk in three months time.

Public Lending Rights (PLR)

Once your book is on library bookshelves, another way of making a small amount of extra money from your book is through public lending rights, which many authors may not have even heard of. In short, Public Lending Right is the right of authors to receive payment for free public use of their works in libraries. When your book is made available in libraries, people may borrow and read it without having to pay for it. To make up for this and intended as a means of supporting of the arts, the government compensates authors for the potential loss of sales. At least 40 countries recognise lending rights in their legislation, but PLR payments occur in only 29 of them, 24 of which are in Europe, fortunately including the UK. There are no PLR systems in France, the United States, South America, Asia or Africa.

Different countries have differing eligibility criteria. In most nations only published works are accepted, government publications are rarely counted, nor are bibliographies or dictionaries. Some PLR payments are made solely to fund literary works of fiction, and some countries like Norway have a sliding scale paying less for non-fiction works. Many nations also exclude scholarly and academic texts.

How the payment amounts are determined also varies between countries. Some pay based on how many times a book has been taken out of a library, others base payment on whether a library owns a book or not. In the UK, payments are based on the number of times your book is borrowed. Details of book loans are collected from a sample of public library computer systems across the country by the PLR office. This data is used to calculate the estimated number of times that books are borrowed nationally, and payment is made on the basis of an annually calculated rate per loan, currently around 6p. You are never going to get rich through PLR payments, but it is good to know when additional monies are due to you for your writing.

To qualify for payment, applicants must register their books with the Public Lending Rights Office (www.plr.uk.com). Payments are made annually on the basis of loans data collected from a sample of public libraries in the UK. Over 23,000 writers, illustrators, photographers, translators and editors receive PLR payments each year. PLR is funded by the Department for Culture, Media and Sport in the UK and in 2008-09, £6.6 million was paid to authors directly into their bank or building society accounts in February of each year.

The Authors' Licensing and Collecting Society (ALCS)

The Authors' Licensing and Collecting Society (ALCS) (www.alcs.co.uk) collects money due to its members from the Copyright Lending Agency (CLA) for secondary uses of their work which includes photocopying, digital reproduction, educational recording and repeat use via the internet. This income is typically made up of small transactions that are difficult for individual writers to monitor, but can be tracked by the ALCS database. To become an ALCS Member you pay a one-off lifetime fee of £25. This is deducted from your first royalty payment so you do not have to pay anything upfront. Also, you will not have to pay anything if they do not collect any money for you.

The ALCS is especially beneficial for authors who write educational material which often gets photocopied and digitally reproduced. ALCS has over 70,000 writer members in the UK and abroad. Payment is made twice a year of any money collected on your behalf, typically in September and February. ALCS charges a commission on all money it pays out to its members. The current rate of commission in 2009 is 9.5% for members, and 14% for non-members.

CHAPTER 16

Festivals, Conferences & Trade Shows

Literary festivals present unique opportunities for authors to meet their readers and publicize their books. Whether organized by chambers of commerce, tourist bureaus, or publishing industry groups, book fairs have the potential to bring authors face-to-face with the reading public. They will also be attended by professional book buyers, publishers, retailers, library representatives and members of the media covering the event. Similarly, a trade show or conference provide a great opportunity to showcase your work, network, make new contacts and keep in touch with existing contacts, learn more about the market for your book, share new ideas and scout out the competition.

Attending Book Fairs

Firstly, you should do some research and list those festivals which you might like to attend. *The Writer's Handbook* by MacMillan provides an excellent list of nearly a hundred literary festivals across the UK. This includes the major literary events like the annual Cheltenham Literature Festival in October sponsored by *The Times* newspaper which is the largest and most popular festival of its kind in Europe, the annual Hay Festival in May sponsored by *The Guardian,* the Bath Literary Festival which has over 100 different literary-related events, and the annual week-long Oxford Literary Festival held in March/April sponsored by *The Sunday Times.*

It lists smaller festivals like the BayLit Festival in Cardiff Bay, the Isle of Man Literature Festival, the Knutsford Literature Festival, Mere Literary Festival, Off the Shelf Literary Festival in Sheffield, Oundle Festival of Literature, Warwick Words, the Wigtown Book Festival in Scotland, and Writing on the Wall in Liverpool. There are specialist book fairs for children's books in Bath and Brighton, and crime festivals such as Theakston's Old Peculier Harrogate Crime Writing Festival and Reading Festival of Crime Writing.

Once you have done your research and drafted a list of festivals that you would like to attend, become a featured author. Most literary festivals have author readings, so you might contact the event organizers in advance and offer to do one or propose a panel discussion, with you as moderator or speaker at the event. Use this opportunity to mention your book in the context of the talk to a captive audience of book aficionados.

At most literary events, individuals can purchase a table and set up their own materials for festival-goers to browse. Contact your publisher to see if they have bought a table or space at the event and if so, suggest a book signing at your publisher's stand and ask if they will help promote your book and contribute towards your travel expenses. Make a large sign with your name and the title of your book prominently displayed. You might have poster of your book's jacket professionally printed and mounted, which you could display on an easel or at the front of your table. You can reuse it at subsequent events.

Work the crowd. Speaking to the public can be easier if you have something to show people. Promotional postcards, which you can make yourself with a home computer and inkjet printer, are a simple way to introduce yourself and your book to passers-by. Once you hand someone something, whether it's a postcard, a bookmark or other promotional item, you have their attention and hopefully their interest. In addition to your hand-outs, have copies of your book with you to sell. Bring a stack of postcards or flyers with you, and search out clusters of people and engage them in conversation. Make eye contact with anyone you hand a flyer or postcard to. Authors can never do enough to publicize their books, and book fairs are an ideal place to raise your profile and build up a readership because you know that those attending have already expressed an interest in books.

Selling Books to the Trade

If your book is specialized in some way and linked to a certain profession, then trade shows, business expos, and other professional events offer excellent opportunities to engage directly with a large number of potential book buyers in a relatively short space of time. Trade fairs enable you to showcase your work and explain its benefits, to build on your existing relationships with clients and book buyers, and also established new contacts within your professional or industry. Exhibiting at a trade fair is one of the best ways to show your book and its practical use in the best possible light. The more effort you put into the planning stage, the more likely you are to get the most for your marketing budget.

Before you decide which trade shows you want to attend and how you want to present yourself and your book, it is worth reflecting on what you hope to achieve. Set clear goals for yourself in terms of how many people you plan to speak to, how many copies of your book you hope to sell. Are you introducing an inspiring or novel idea in your book, positioning yourself as an authority and your book as an authoritative source within the market, or focusing primarily on generating new sales and new customers for your own business? You should set reachable targets and try to surpass them.

Contact trade associations and related professional organizations that can provide you with a comprehensive list of events, locations and dates. If you prefer to identify specific markets in which to exhibit, get in touch with area chambers of commerce or event organizers such as www.exhibitions.co.uk to locate forthcoming events in a particular area. The internet offers a range of information for locating relevant events and some sites provide extensive trade show databases with a targeted search capacity. Find out how many people are likely to attend and how they might match your target audience. Determine how long the exhibition has been running and what kind of reputation it has within the industry. Check on how and where the event is being advertised, as this is generally a good indication of the show's suitability for your work.

Before registering, ask the organizers whether you can sell copies of your book at the fair, as some shows do not allow direct sales. Stand space at large trade shows can be fairly expensive, so you need to be confident that you will see a reasonable return on your investment. If you have not done so already, it might be worthwhile attending a few trade shows beforehand, to get a feel for how they are organized and what kinds of books are generally exhibited, and which types of displays seems to be most effective.

If you do decide to pay for a stand, start with a small stand and see how it goes. Smaller regional events typically are less expensive and more cost-effective. Make sure that your stand will fit the space you are buying at each show. Ask whether you want the same size stand for each show, depending on the profile of those attending and the demand you think your stand is likely to create. Whether you are planning an exhibit for one or numerous trade fairs, you want to make the best use of the stand you create and your time at the fair.

Ask the event organizer for a list of attendees and send a mail-out telling them what your work is about and where to find you at the exhibition or event. You might tell them that you will be signing copies of your book at the trade fair, and offering a special discount of 20% off the purchase price for your book at the fair for anyone bringing copies of your mail-out to the table. Also make sure your current readers or others within your profession on your mailing list know that you will be there and invite them along as well.

Create an interesting and welcoming stand that is inviting and encourages people to stop, browse, introduce themselves to you and ask questions. Use an eye-catching banner, easel or poster with the front cover of your book professionally printed and mounted and prominently display to draw people in. Your stand should also have co-ordinated colours and a clean, professional look. While there are stands to fit every budget, it does not pay to cut corners – remember, your trade show stand reflects the professionalism of your writing, and the promotional material you use can be used again, so it is worth the investment.

Many trade show attendees will come to your stand to browse and then move on to the next thing. Try to catch their eye and engage them briefly in conversation, perhaps asking them if there is anything you can help them with. The more you time you have to take an interest in the attendees themselves, making them feel invited and comfortable, the more effective you will be. There are obviously peak hours and days at any trade fair, and you want to be sure that you are not on your lunch break or away from your stand at the busiest times of the day.

When someone expresses an interest in you or your book, ask them to give you their details such as name, job title and company. These will help you form a database of potential book buyers who you can follow-up with after the show with information about your next book, and giving them your website or blog details.

Conferences, Conventions, Workshops, Seminars and Other Venues

These events, like book fairs and trade shows, typically draw people with a particular interest. For example if you've had written an educational coursebook, conventions are a good chance to you speak with other educators about your book and possibly including it in their recommended reading lists or class discussions. Some of these events, especially writers' workshops, are directed at a very specific niche market. If your book occupies that niche in some way, attendance and speaking engagements can be especially beneficial in raising your profile and selling more copies of your book.

Conferences and conventions come is all shapes and sizes, and this is reflected in the cost of attending. The larger the event, the more likely you are to benefit by speaking, chairing or participating in a panel discussion. The smaller the event, the more likely you are to benefit by personal interaction with those participating, as you will have a much more targeted attendee list, and thus a better opportunity to reach your core readership.

Depending on the nature and subject matter of your book, there may be other venues which offer you promotional opportunities. If you have written a children's adventure story, you might mention your book at meetings for Scouts, Guides, Cubs, Rainbows and Brownies. If you have written a self-help or dieting book, then there may be various organizations in your community which would welcome a talk from you about your book and how it might benefit them. If you work as a professional karate teacher and you have written book about the history of your sport, or the principles and background to your teaching, then each of the sporting venues where you teach are ideal for setting up a stall and selling your book.

Wasyl Kolesnikov, an internationally recognized mind and body development teacher, published *Return to the Source* and *Transformation: A Spiritual Journey into Yourself* based on his teaching practices in Aikido and Tai Chi, both of which he sold to current students and prospect students at various sporting centres. The books give him even more authority as an inspirational Sensei, and his teaching role helps to sell more books. This is the ideal situation for any author writing about a particular perspective, practice or professional.

CHAPTER 17

Guerrilla Marketing & Book Sharing

This is where your creative talents come into play again, and where your personal drive to succeed as an author can take you to new heights. Sometime you need to think outside the bookstore box and think up new ways to capture public attention and support for your book. The term "guerrilla marketing" was coined and defined by Jay Conrad Levinson as an unconventional way of performing marketing activities on a low budget, relying more on time, energy and imagination rather than a big marketing spend. Typically, guerrilla marketing campaigns are unexpected and unconventional, and consumers are targeted in unexpected places. The objective of guerrilla marketing is to create a unique, engaging and thought-provoking concept to generate a buzz for what you are trying to sell, and consequently turn viral either off-line (word of mouth) or on-line (word of mouse).

Authors often use guerrilla marketing techniques to break into the market and create a buzz about their book. Many new authors do not have the financial resources required to sustain a lengthy marketing campaign, especially when they have spent a lot their time recently in writing, publishing and promoting their book rather than in full-time employment. Thus, they have to be entrepreneurial and imaginative in their approach to marketing to stand out from the madding crowd.

There are authors prepared to read their book at the top of Mount Everest to garner publicity, or ride through the streets of Coventry in true Lady Godiva style to raise awareness, and a few eyebrows, of their book. Basketball star Dennis Rodman showed up in a wedding dress to promote his new book. An Indonesian businessman named Tung Desem Waringin circled a soccer field in Serang dumping bags of cash to promote his new book. However, these are extreme cases, and one does not have go to such audacious heights, dress in bizarre clothing, or throw money at people to creatively market their book.

Rick Warren recently penned a book entitled *The Hope You Need*. To gain pre-release publicity for his book, he announced via Twitter to his 43,342 followers that they could design the cover for his new book. The design contest for the book cover was hosted on 99designs.com, and his publisher offered a monetary prize for the winning book design. Over 3,500 book cover designs were submitted, and there are now dozens of blogs and articles devoted to his book.

Don Miller hid manuscripts of his book *A Million Miles in a Thousand Years* in tour stops and cities across the country. Each day, Thomas Nelson sent messages via Twitter and Facebook with information on the location of 2 of the 60 "bootleg" copies of the book. Each person who found a copy of the manuscript was given Don Miller's mobile phone number to call and talk with him.

Kevin Joslin, author of *See John Run* (2009), which is a humorous collection of BBC Radio 2 stories as read by Terry Wogan, discussed running a national competition on Twitter in conjunction with his publisher to include the name of the competition reader in one of his naughtily hilarious Janet and John parodies.

The common link in each of these creative promotional activities is the use of social networking sites (as discussed in Chapter 10) to spread the word and hook readers into participating in their competitions. You can do this on a smaller scale by inviting a UK book club to run a contest on your book, or perhaps twittering your local newspaper, and asking your publisher or a local business to fund or sponsor the prize, even if that prize is a few complimentary copies of your book signed by you as the esteemed author.

Youtube (as discussed in Chapter 11) offers another excellent opportunity to think of unconventional and creative ways to promote your book. James Patterson produced a Youtube video for his book *I, Alex Cross* in which he says he will "kill off Alex Cross if you do not buy copies of his book." In other words, you the reader will kill off Alex Cross if you do not buy copies of his book. Similarly, Chris Anderson's innovative and stylish promotional video for his *Long Tail* has been nominated for various awards for its creativity. My personal favourites are the Youtube videos for *Tales of Mere Existence* by Yev Yilmaz and *Simon's Cat* by Simon Tofield.

As part of your imaginative marketing campaign, factor in how you will tell the media about what you are doing. There's no point going to all that trouble, and simply hoping that they will hear about it and consider worth covering. Summarize in a short press release what you will be doing, where and when, and let the media know so editors and journalists can see that it will be worth covering.

You should be wary about organizing a publicity campaign that may go wrong, get out of control, or get you into trouble, exposing you and your publisher to potential litigation. At the Frankfurt Book Fair in 2009, Eichborn, a German publisher whose logo is a fly, attached notes to 200 flies who flew around the room promoting their book stand. They claim their books flew off the shelves, but there has also been some negative response to the idea of tying notes to animals to promote books, and the Book Fair organisers did not find the stunt funny, releasing 200 banner-clad flies into their convention centre with food stalls and hygiene standards, as they felt it "flied in the face of convention" and "booklovers do not attend the Book Fair just to be pestered by branded insects."

As Levinson says in *The Guerrilla Marketing Handbook*, "In order to sell a product or a service, a company must establish a relationship with the customer. It must build trust and support. It must understand the customer's needs, and it must provide a product that delivers the promised benefits." Gimmicks do not achieve this, results do. And relationship-building is essential in building a readership for your book. It is not good enough just to be memorable. You need to be remembered in a good way for any marketing campaign to be successful and for you to profit from your writing.

Book Sharing

People who love books enjoy sharing their favourite book with others once they have finished with them, rather than having the taking up space and gathering dust on their bookshelves at home. One way to do this is by what is known as Book Crossing, which is "a novel idea" where you leave your book on a park bench, a coffee shop, museum, doctor's office, or in a hotel room on vacation, the idea being that it might find a new reader or new home where it will be read and enjoyed again. What happens next is up to fate. You never know where our book might travel, unless, as do many avid book crossers, you leave your first name, town and date the book on the inside cover which gives your book a wonderful, "I was there" type feel to it, much like a message in a bottle or a time capsule.

There are Book Crossing groups and websites specifically set up to encourage book sharing in this way, as it is also environmentally-friendly. According to the Eco-Libris website and based on a report published in March 2008 on "Environmental Trends and Climate Impact" prepared by The Green Press Initiative (GPI) and The Book Industry Study Group (BISG), over 30 million trees are cut down annually for the production of books sold in the United States alone! Rather than cutting down trees to print more books, why not share the ones that you have which are already in print with others. By recycling reads in this way, bibliophiles can breathe life into their favourite books and send them on an adventure of their own, releasing (or treeleasing) it into the wild.

If you join BookCrosser.com which over 800,000 others in over 130 countries have done since it was launched in April 2001 by Ron Hornbaker, you can track a book's journey around the world as it is passed on from person to person. Over 6 million books have been registered on the site. There are also interesting forums to discuss your favorite authors, characters and books in every genre throughout history right up through current releases. Dan Brown's *The Da Vinci*

Code is the most crossed book, followed by Yann Martel's *Life Of Pi*. The top ten includes *To Kill A Mockingbird* by Harper Lee and *The Five People You Meet In Heaven* by Mitch Albom.

Bookhopper.com enables people to share their passion for books by mailing them to other book hoppers who have expressed an interest in reading and receiving their book. If you have received a number of complimentary copies of your book from your publisher, this may be an excellent opportunity for you to get your book reviewed if send it to book hoppers who might be linked to the media. Alternatively, ask them in your mailing if they would kindly review the book on a specific book review website for you, telling them that you are the author of the book.

Sharing-books.com does much the same for children's books, albeit on a smaller scale, in partnership with Room to Read (www.roomtoread.org), which is a global organization providing books for underprivileged children and building libraries throughout the work in developing countries.

The first Book Crossing UK Unconvention! was even held in Edinburgh in July 2009, sponsored by Word Press and a number of traditional publishers.

If you decided to self-publish your book and included in the publishing package was fifty or more complimentary copies of your book, many of which still sit in the box in which they arrived because you have already donated a few copies to you local libraries, then you might consider book crossing or hopping with them. If your novel finds its way around the world to exotic places, which you can track on the Book Crossing website, then this in itself could be the basis for a good news story, and the more your book has travelled, the wider the appeal.

And finally.....

Any marketing campaign will need to be tailored to your own book, and the success of your promotional activities will depend on careful planning and the time, energy and creativity you are prepared to devote to it. Nobody is going to be able to do everything in this book to sell their book. Rather, you should focus on those activities that you feel you can do and will do, and devote your time and energy to them. In terms of creativity, you have already shown that you are creative by writing a book and if you are a good storyteller, a good raconteur so to speak, then you can think of even more interesting and fun ways to promote your book.

For example, you might get copies of your book cover or website/blog address printed onto t-shirts, calendars or coffee mugs and hand them out to people at your publisher's book stand at the London Book Fair. You might donate signed copies of your book at a school raffle, or sell signed copies of your book on eBay. You might host a writer's workshop or book reading evenings, or distribute bookmarks personally to readers in your local library. I know one author who sells hampers and included a copy of his book in each hamper, subtly passing on the price of the book in the cost of the hamper.

If you are feeling particularly ambitious, you might run an advertisement at your local movie theatre, or you could host your own "whodunit" mystery night if your book is a mystery or crime thriller. Whatever your marketing plans are, make sure that you can carry them off without disappointing or upsetting participants, your readers, other authors, event organizers, and so on. Check with retailers and business owners before you distribute promotional material on their premises.

Whatever you do or your publisher does in terms of selling and marketing your book reflects on you as an author, and the more professional and respectful of others you can be, the more likely they will take an avid interest in what you have to say and write. Most importantly, enjoy the journey from beginning to end. You can be proud of your book and all that you have done in bringing it to market and giving it every chance of success.

GLOSSARY OF TERMS

Amazon.com: The leading online retailer of books in the world today.

Authors' Licensing and Collecting Society (ALCS): Collects money due to author members for secondary uses of their work which includes photocopying, digital reproduction, educational recording and repeat use via the internet.

Banner Ad: Graphic advertisement used to advertise on websites.

Bebo.com: An acronym for "Blog Early, Blog Often". Bebo is a social networking site different from others in that it has a section dedicated to writers called *Bebo Authors*.

Blog (short for *Web log*): Online journal or news site updated regularly and reflecting the author's interests and current activities.

Book Channel: The processes and services involved in taking a book from the publisher to readers.

Book-Crossing: The act of leaving your book in a public place so that it might find a new reader or new home where it will be read and enjoyed again.

Book Endorsement: Written testimonials to the quality of your book often provide by people who are well-known and respected.

Bookfinder.com: An online directory of internet retailers selling your book.

Book-Hopping: Sharing your passion for books by mailing them to others who have expressed an interest in reading and receiving the book.

Book Launch: An organized event at which you announce and celebrate the publication of your book.

Book Return Program: An arrangement between a retailer and author or publisher by which books are ordered and stocked by the retailer on a "sell or return" basis.

Book Review: A written commentary on your book by someone who has read it.

Book Signing: An event in which an author signs copies of his books for readers and fans, often after a short reading and question-and-answer session.

Book Tour: A series of events attended by authors in which they promote their book with speaking engagements and book signings.

Demographics: Recognizable characteristics of a group of consumers, including age, gender, income, education, location, interests, and so on.

Direct Marketing: Sending and selling your book directly to readers and retailers, typically through e-mail, telephone, post or fax.

Distribution: Marketing and supplying books directly to readers and retailers.

Domain Name/URL (uniform research locator): The internet address for your website, generally beginning with http://www or simply www. and ending with .com, .co.uk, .net., .org, and so on.

E-Commerce: Online selling, typically involving the acceptance of credit card details, site security for online transactions, and an order fulfilment process in place.

Facebook.com: A social networking website on which you can add friends to your Facebook page and send them messages, alerting them as often as you would like about new events in your life, such as the publication of your book.

Gardners: The UK largest book wholesaler. Waterstone's, the UK's leading retailer, buys all their books from small publishers via Gardners.

Gather.com: A social networking website designed to encourage interaction through various social, political and cultural topics.

Guerrilla Marketing: An unconventional way of performing promotional activities on a low budget, relying more on time, energy and imagination than a big marketing spend.

ISBN (International Standard Book Number): A unique and internationally recognized 13-digit identification number assigned to a book.

Lovereading.com: The largest UK book club on the internet and along with its partner site, Lovewriting.com, offers advice on publishing your work, and makes it easy for people to sample, review and purchase your book.

Marketing Campaign: The activities you undertake to raise your profile as a published author and promote and sell copies of your book.

Marketing Plan: A written document setting out your aims, expectation, strategy and targets for selling your book to readers and retailers.

Market Research: The careful gathering and analysis of information about your reader's interests and buying habits as well as competition from other books so you can target readers and book buyers for sales most effectively.

Media Kit / Press Pack: A collection of marketing materials including a press release, author brief, fact sheet about your book, current news, suggested interview Q & As and your contact details which can be sent to the media to publicize your book.

MySpace.com: A social networking website with an interactive, user-submitted network of friends, personal profiles, blogs, groups, photos and music.

Niche Market: Narrow and closely defined areas of a target audience that share a particular need, idea, or interest related to a specific product or service. *Niche retailers* are those whose products or services cater to a niche market.

Nielsen BookData: Provides up-to-date book sales and market information to retailers, libraries and publishers in over 100 countries worldwide.

Nielsen Bookscan: Collects retail sales information from point of sale systems in more than 33,500 bookshops around the world. Publishers use this information to check on the success of their books and organize further print runs for books, while libraries and bookshops use the date to decide which books to order in.

Ning.com: A social networking site enabling you to create your *own* social networking site based on a particular subject.

Offset printing: Conventional printing method whereby plates bearing the book's pages images are prepared, and set-up costs are the same irrespective of how many books are printed.

Pay-per-click (PPC) advertising: A form of advertising where you bid on specific key words and key word phrases relevant to your website so when someone puts those words into an internet search engine, banners and links are provided to your website. Each time someone clicks on these banners or links and are directed to your website, you pay a small fee to the PPC advertiser.

Podcasting: Recording videos and making them available to anyone with a Broadband (speedy) internet connection.

Press Release: Short (typically one or two pages) announcement of newsworthy events associated with your book.

Print-On-Demand (POD): Modern printing technique where books are saved in portable document format (PDF) and printed off a computer. They can thereby be printed one at a time, once they have actually been ordered and paid for.

PR websites / Newswires: Distributors for press releases on the internet.

Publicist: Someone who is paid to help promote your book.

Public Lending Rights (PLR): The right of authors to receive payment for free public use of their works in libraries.

Reciprocal links: A mutual link between your website and another website intended to increase the numbers of visitors to both sites, and thereby achieve higher ranking on search engines, giving your site more prominence.

Sale or Return: Trading arrangement in which a seller sends books to a buyer or reseller who pays the author or rights holder only as and when the goods are sold. The author or publisher agrees to take back any unsold books (called "returns") after an agreed period of time, often 90 days.

Search Engine Optimization: Tailoring your website so that when people search online for subjects related to your book on various browsers such like Google and Yahoo, they might find and access your website.

Social Networking: Expanding the number of one's contacts by making connections through other individuals. On the internet, establishing interconnected communities (commonly known as personal networks) that help people make contacts that would be good for them to know, but that they would be unlikely to have met otherwise.

Spamming: Bulk distribution of advertising information, typically through e-mail or fax.

Target Market: A group of people identified as those most likely to buy your book.

The Self Publishing Magazine: UK print magazine offering information, advice and case studies about self-published books. The magazine also incorporates the *Readers' Review Magazine* which publishes independent reviews of self-published books.

The Self-Publishing Review: An online magazine with self-publishing news and reviews. It is also a social network where writers, readers, and publishers can connect and share ideas.

Trade Fair (Trade Show or Expo): An exhibition organized so that companies in a specific industry can showcase and demonstrate their latest products and service, study the activities of competitors and examine recent trends and opportunities.

Twitter.com: A free web-based service enabling its users to send and read messages short messages to one another known as *tweets* via the Twitter website, text-messaging or other external applications.

Video blogging (vlogging or vidblogging): A form of blogging where short videos are made regularly and often combine embedded video or a video link with supporting text, images, and other data.

Viral Marketing: An unconventional way of performing marketing activities on a low budget, relying more on time, energy and imagination than a big marketing spend.

Website: A collection of information, images, and other content accessed online through a specific internet address.

Website Hosting: Reserving a space on the internet which enables you to have your own pages on the world wide web (www.)

Word of Mouse Marketing: Using social networking sites on the internet to create a buzz about your book.

Word of Mouth Marketing: Speaking with people and groups of people directly to create a following for your book.

YouTube: A video sharing website on which users can upload, share and view videos.

www.ingramcontent.com/pod-product-compliance
Lightning Source LLC
Chambersburg PA
CBHW022252290526
45785CB00015B/720